AF600151

PAROCHIAL SUBSTITUTE VICARS AND SUPPLYING PRIESTS

The Catholic University of America
Canon Law Studies
No. 265

PAROCHIAL SUBSTITUTE VICARS AND SUPPLYING PRIESTS

A COMMENTARY WITH HISTORICAL NOTES

BY

Urban S. Wagner, O.F.M.Conv., J.C.L.
PRIEST OF THE ORDER OF FRIARS
MINOR CONVENTUAL

PROVINCE OF OUR LADY OF CONSOLATION

A DISSERTATION
Submitted to the Faculty of the School of Canon Law of the Catholic University of America in Partial Fulfillment of the Requirements for the Degree of Doctor of Canon Law

THE CATHOLIC UNIVERSITY OF AMERICA PRESS
WASHINGTON, D. C.
1947

Nihil Obstat:

CLEMENS R. ORTH, O.F.M. CONV., J.C.D.
Censor Deputatus

Ludovicopoli, die 15 iulii 1947

Imprimi Potest:

ANTONIUS HODAPP, O.F.M., CONV.
Minister Provincialis

Ludovicopoli, die 18 iulii 1947

Nihil Obstat:

CLEMENS V. BASTNAGEL, J.U.D.

Censor Deputatus

Washingtonii, die 21 iulii 1947

Imprimatur:

✠ CAROLUS J. ALTER, D.D.

Episcopus Dioecesis Toletanae in America

Toletana in America, die 25 iulii 1947

The Wickersham Printing Co.
Lancaster, Penna.

FOREWORD

The first consideration of the Church has always been that each and every member of the faith should receive full and proper pastoral care at all times. Since it is beneficial and useful for the pastor of a church to enjoy the option of an absence from his parish at stated times, diligent care is taken by the Church lest the needs of the faithful be neglected during such absences of the pastor. To guard against this possible neglect the office of the parochial substitute vicar and the position of the supplying priest were instituted in the Church.

The priest who takes the place of a pastor who will be absent from his parish for over a week is called a substitute vicar precisely because he is taking the place of the pastor and rules the parish, not in his own name, but in the name of the pastor. The supplying priest is the priest who takes the place of a pastor who will be absent from his parish for less than a week.

Since the substitute vicar takes the place of the pastor in all things, and since he possesses an ecclesiastical office in the strict sense, the greater part of this dissertation deals with his rights and duties in regard to the spiritual care of the parishioners entrusted to him. An endeavor is made to specify and to particularize his rights and obligations as much as possible. Since but little has been written on the rights and duties of the substitute vicar, the dissertation must often fall back upon the analogy that exists between the office of substitute and the office of pastor. No separate historical treatment is included inasmuch as the office of substitute vicar, as such, did not exist prior to the present Code of Canon Law.

The supplying priest who takes the place of a pastor who will be absent from his parish for less than a week holds no ecclesiastical office and consequently possesses no special rights or duties. The mandate of the pastor and not the general law of the Code is his guiding norm.

The writer at this time expresses his gratitude to the Very Rev. Anthony Hodapp, O. F. M. Conv., Minister Provincial, for the opportunity of completing his graduate studies in Canon Law. At the same time he expresses his gratitude to the Faculty of the School of Canon Law at the Catholic University of America for their untiring attention and assistance, to the Librarian of the University Library for her repeated acts of helpfulness and courtesy, and to all who aided him in the final preparation of this text.

TABLE OF CONTENTS

CHAPTER III

CHAPTER IV

CHAPTER V

CHAPTER VI

CHAPTER VII

CHAPTER I

Preliminary Considerations

ARTICLE 1. NOMENCLATURE

Etymologically the word *vicarius* points to one *qui vicem alicuius gerit.*[1] It is not a new term in law; it is one which was used extensively by the old Roman jurists.[2] It is known, for instance, that Constantine the Great (306-337) divided the Roman Empire into four prefectures, each prefecture having a praetor in charge. These prefectures were again divided into dioceses with a vicar prefect at the head of each diocese. The dioceses in turn were subdivided into provinces, which were headed by rectors.[3] It was a very logical development, therefore, that the term " vicar " should be taken into ecclesiastical law to designate one who was taking the place of another.[4]

Among the different kinds of vicars mentioned in the earlier law one finds vicars who were appointed by the Apostolic See [5] and vicars, especially archpriests and archdeacons, who were appointed by the bishops.[6] At a later

---

[1] Cf. Forcellini, *Totius Latinitatis Lexicon* (6 vols., Prati: Typis Aldinianis, 1858-1860), ad v. *Vicarius.*

[2] Cf. C. (1.38) throughout, where the office of vicar is defined.

[3] Cf. Wernz, *Ius Decretalium* (6 vols., Vol. II, 3. ed., Prati, 1915) II, n. 545, ad IV.

[4] Cf. Pius VI, *Responsio ad Metropolitanas Moguntinum, Trevirensem, Coloniensem, Salisburgensem super Nunciaturis Apostolicis* (Romae, 1789), cap. 8.

[5] Cf. Pius VI, *Responsio, loc. cit.;* cc. 3, 4, x, *de officio legati,* I, 30; Wernz, *Ius Decretalium,* II, n. 545.

[6] Cf. Wernz, *Ius Decretalium,* II, n. 545, ad IV; X, *de officio archidiaconi,* I, 23; Ojetti, *Synopsis Rerum Moralium et Iuris Pontificii* (3 ed., 3 vols. and Index, Romae, 1909-1914) ad v. *archidiaconus* (hereafter cited as *Synopsis*).

date, too, the bishops began to appoint vicars general.[7] It was only a natural development, therefore, that pastors and others who were given the care of souls should also have their vicars.

In the pre-Code law "parochial vicars", that is, the ones who temporarily or permanently took the place of the pastor in the administration of the parish,[8] were defined by Wernz (1842-1914) as ". . . *illi presbyteri, qui vices agunt alicuius parochi in exercitio curae animarum.*"[9] As the word itself indicates, the vicar was not simply the helper (*adiutor*) of the pastor. He was the one who took the place of the pastor when the latter was absent.[10]

In the pre-Code law, the temporary vicar, that is, the one who took the place of the pastor for a time only, could be appointed for a variety of reasons. Among them may be mentioned the infirmity of the pastor, the inability of the pastor to speak the language of the people, the absence of the pastor for the recovery of his health, or for the making of a pilgrimage to some shrine, and the like.[11] The pastor, however, was not perfectly free to leave his parish

[7] Cf. c. 1, *de officio vicarii,* I, 13, in VI°; Ojetti, *Synopsis,* ad v. *Vicarius generalis;* Wernz, *Ius Decretalium,* II, n. 804 ff.

[8] Cf. *Glossa ordinaria* ad c. un., *de officio vicarii,* I, 7, in Clem., ad v. *perpetuis.*

[9] *Ius Decretalium,* II, n. 837. Cf. Bouix, *Tractatus de Parocho* (3 ed., Parisiis, 1880), pp. 417 ff.; Santi, *Praelectiones Iuris Canonici* (2 vols., Ratisbonae, Neo-Eboraci, Cincinnati, 1886), Lib. I, tit. 28.

[10] Cf. Raus, *Institutiones Canonicae* (editio altera et emendata, Vitte: Parisiis, 1931), n. 162.

[11] Cf. Schmalzgrueber, *Jus Ecclesiasticum Universum* (5 vols. in 12, Romae: 1843-1845), Lib. I, tit. 28, n. 7, ad 1-6 (hereafter cited *Jus Ecclesiasticum*). Other reasons which sufficed for the constituting of a temporary vicar are listed in Schmalzgrueber, *Jus Ecclesiasticum, loc. cit.;* Reiffenstuel, *Jus Canonicum Universum* (5 vols in 7, Parisiis, 1735), Lib. I, tit. 28, n. 47 (hereafter cited *Jus Canonicum*). Cf. also Pirhing, *Jus Canonicum Nova Methodo Explicatum* (5 vols. in 4, Dilingae, 1674-1678), Lib. I, tit. 28, n. 18 (hereafter cited *Jus Canonicum*).

as he pleased. The reason for his absence had to be approved by the bishop.[12]

The need underlying the appointment of a temporary vicar becomes apparent when the mind of the Council of Trent regarding the residence of pastors and of the rectors of churches is examined.

> Cum praecepto divino mandatum sit omnibus, quibus animarum cura commissa est, oves suas agnoscere, pro his sacrificium offerre, verbique divini praedicatione, sacramentorum administratione, ac bonorum omnium operum exemplo pascere pauperum aliarumque miserabilium personarum curam paternam gerere, et in cetera munia pastoralia incumbere; quae omnia nequaquam ab iis praestari et impleri possunt, qui gregi suo non invigilant neque assistunt, sed mercenariorum more deserunt: sacrosancta Synodus eos admonet, et hortatur, ut divinorum praeceptorum memores, factique forma gregis, in iudicio, et veritate pascunt, et regunt.[13]

This same Council determined that anyone who did not fulfill the law of residence was to be deprived of the fruits of his benefice, which were then to be given to the poor.[14] And if the pastor was contumacious in his refusal to reside at his parish, he was to be punished by the bishop with ecclesiastical censures, and even to be deprived of his office.[15] The same obligation of residence in his parish rests upon the pastor since the promulgation of the present

---

[12] Conc. Trident., sess VII, *de ref., c.* 2. Cf. Reiffenstuel, *Jus Canonicum,* Lib. I, tit. 28, n. 52; Pirhing, *Jus Canonicum,* Lib. I, tit. 28, n. 21; Barbosa, *Iuris Ecclesiastici Universi Libri Tres* (Lugduni: 1660), Lib. III, c. 6, n. 63 (hereafter cited *Ius Ecclesiasticum*).

[13] Conc. Trident., sess. XXIII, *de ref.,* c. 1.

[14] Conc. Trident., *loc. cit.* Cf. c. 15, *de rescriptis,* I, 3, in VI°.

[15] Conc. Trident., *loc. cit.* Cf. also c. 11, X, *de clericis non residentibus,* III, 4.

Code of Canon Law.[16] And the same penalties can be threatened against a pastor who refuses to reside in his parish.[17]

In this matter, however, as in all her regulations, the Church is reasonable. The pastor is allowed by law to take a vacation every year.[18] The universal law also obliges a cleric to make a spiritual retreat at least once every three years which normally requires the pastor to be absent from his parish.[19] The pastor, therefore, is permitted to be away from his parish at certain times. But the obligation to see that the souls entrusted to his care continue to receive the pastoral care that is due them remains intact. It was precisely because of this need that canon 474 was put into the the Code:

> *Vicarius substitutus qui constituitur ad normam can. 465, §§ 4, 5 et can. 1923, § 2, locum parochi tenet in omnibus quae ad curam animarum spectant, nisi Ordinarius loci vel parochus aliquid exceperint.*[20]

---

16 Can. 465, § 1. It must be remembered, however, that the bishop can allow a pastor to live outside of his parish as long as there is a just cause and the parishioners suffer no harm.

17 Cf. cans. 2168-2175.

18 Can. 465, § 2. For a more thorough discussion of this point cf. *infra* pp. 5 ff.

19 Can. 126. All religious, however, are bound to make a retreat every year according to can. 595, 1°. The III Plenary Council of Baltimore (1884) in n. 75 made the following regulation: "*Statuimus itaque ut Episcopi clerum suarum diocesium quotannis vel saltem singulis bienniis in sacrum istum secessum ducant . . .*" This obligation is still effective though it binds the bishops directly whereas the provision of canon 126 is directly binding on the clergy.

20 Even though the Code in can. 465, §§ 4, 5, distinguishes the substitute vicar, who is appointed in the regular manner (cf. *infra*, pp. 32, fn. 54, ff.), from the supplying priest, who is appointed in an urgent case, the latter is, and as Vermeersch-Creusen point out, can be called, a substitute vicar. (*Epitome Iuris Canonici* [3 vols., Vol. 1, 6 ed., Mechliniae, Romae: H.

ART 2. CIRCUMSTANCES WHICH OCCASION THE APPOINTMENT

As has already been indicated, the pre-Code law demanded that one who had charge of souls had to obtain the services of a temporary vicar before he could leave his parish for any length of time.[21] This arrangement was incumbent upon the pastor under threat of penalty.[22] The present Code follows the same policy [23] in order to safeguard the right that the faithful have to a permanent ministry.

There are, however, four sets of circumstances that can occasion a pastors's departure from his parish. A discussion of these different sets of circumstances will constitute the subject matter of this present article.

A. The Pastor's Vacation

The first case is found in the reading of canon 465, § 4, to which canon 474 refers.

> *Sive continuum sive intermissum sit vacationum tempus, cum absentia ultra hebdomadam est duratura, parochus, praeter legitimam causam, habere debet Ordinarii scriptam licentiam et vicarium substitutum sui loco relinquere ab eodem Ordinario probandum; quod si parochus sit religiosus, indiget praeterea consensu Superioris et substitutus tum ab Ordinario tum a Superiore probari debet.*

Dessain, 1937], I, n. 565—hereafter cited *Epitome*). During the course of this study the term "substitute vicar" will refer to the priest who takes the place of the pastor for over a week, regardless of the way he is appointed: the term "supplying priest" will be used in designation of the priest who takes the place of the pastor for less than a week.

[21] Cf. Schmalzgrueber, *Jus Ecclesiasticum,* Lib. I, tit. 28, nn, 1-6.

[22] Conc. Trident., sess. XXIII, *de ref.,* c. l.

[23] Cf. can. 465. §§ 4, 5.

The term "pastor" in this text is to be taken in the broad sense to include also the quasi-pastor, the actual vicar, the administrator of a parish and even the *vicarii adiutores* who supply for the pastor in all things.[24]

Each year the pastor is allowed a two months' vacation [25] consisting either of one continuous absence or of several absences for shorter periods of time.[26] But even this rule admits of exceptions, since the ordinary, for a just cause, may lengthen or shorten the vacation period.[27] If the pastor were to extend his vacation over the course of the year, taking, for instance, a ten days' leave on six different occasions, he would need to secure the services of a substitute each time he took such a part of his vacation.[28] The same assertion holds true in regard to the spiritual retreat that is required by law. Although the retreat is not counted as part of the pastor's vacation period,[29] he is obliged to secure the services of a substitute vicar if the retreat lasts over a week.

[24] Can. 451, §§ 1, 2. Cf. Toso, *Ad Codicem Iuris Canonici Commentaria Minora* (5 vols., Romae: Marietti, 1920-1927), IV, 125-126.

[25] Computed according to the norms set forth in can. 34, § 2.

[26] Can. 465, § 2.

[27] Can. 465, § 2.

[28] Canon, 465, § 2, must not be misconstrued to mean that a pastor may leave his parish for a day or two many times during the course of the year and still be entitled to his regular two months' vacation period. Beste (*Introductio in Codicem* [ed. altera, Collegeville, Minn.: St. John's Abbey Press, 1944]—hereafter cited *Introductio*) explicitly states that the contrary is true. Cf. also Vermeersch-Creusen, *Epitome*, I, n. 552 ad 2; Ayrinhac, *Constitution of the Church* (London, New York, Toronto: Longmans, Green and Co., 1930), n. 277. An absence of but a few hours during the day, however, is not counted as part of the vacation, according to the principle, *parum pro nihilo reputatur*. Cf. Vermeersch-Creusen, *Epitome, loc. cit.;* Beste, *Introductio, loc. cit.;* Cappello, *Summa Iuris Canonici* (3 vols., Vol. I, 3 ed., Taurini: Marietti, 1938), n. 526, ad 3 (hereafter cited *Summa*.)

[29] Can. 126.

This special point is stressed in canon 465, § 4, namely, whenever a pastor is absent from his parish for over a week (*ultra hebdomadam*), a substitute vicar must be appointed to take his place. Just how is the term *ultra hebdomadam* to be interpreted? Must it be construed to include an absence of just seven days, as, for instance, from Sunday to Sunday? Or is it possible that it may be unnecessary for the pastor to secure the services of a substitute vicar even though he may be away for eight days?

To answer this question one must examine the wording of canon 474, which treats of the appointment of the substitute vicar. There it is explicitly stated that the appointment is to take place according to the norms of canons 465, §§ 4, 5. In these two canons the wording is identical: a vicar must be appointed whenever the pastor's absence is *ultra hebdomadam.* How then is the word *ultra* to be interpreted? In accordance with the rule stated in canon 18, the word must be accepted according to its proper signification. Therefore one may conclude that if a pastor will be absent for exactly one week, a substitute vicar cannot be appointed.[30] But if a pastor will be absent for over one week, for instance, eight days, a substitute vicar must be appointed.[31]

B. *Unexpected Absence for a Grave Cause*

The second case that calls for the appointment of a substitute vicar is stated in canon 465, § 5.

> *Si parochus repentina et gravi de causa discedere atque ultra hebdomadam cogatur abesse, quamprimum per litteras Ordinarium commonefaciat, ei indicans causam discessus et sacerdotem supplentem, eiusque stet mandatis.*

---

[30] Cf. *infra*, p. 34, fn. 59.

[31] Cf. Cappello, " De Vicario Substituto ",—*Periodica,* XIX (1930), 5.

The main difficulty here is to determine the exact and precise meaning of an "unexpected and grave cause." Perhaps the difficulty can best be solved through a consideration of several cases which will illustrate the point at issue.

The pastor of a country parish is notified on a Wednesday morning that one of his parents who lives in a distant city is very ill and that he should come home at once. Because of the distance involved and the nature of the illness the pastor knows that he will not be able to return to his parish for at least ten days (Saturday of the following week).

There is neither any doubt that the cause of his leaving is unexpected, nor that the reason for it is a grave and serious one. Hence the pastor can feel perfectly free to secure the services of a substitute vicar according to the norms given in the canon, and then leave the parish in his charge.[32]

A second possible case is one in which a pastor knows beforehand that one of his parents is to undergo a very serious operation on a particular day, let it be called the fifteenth of May. But, since he is preparing the school children for their first Holy Communion and is planning to redecorate the church, the matter completely slips his mind. Then, on the fourteenth of May he receives a letter which reminds him that he is expected to be home before the operation. The pastor knows that he will have to be away from the parish for over a week. He knows too that he had sufficient time to secure the services of a substitute in the regular manner. Now he wonders whether the cause of his contemplated absence is actually "*repentina*" in his case.

---

[32] Cf. Claeys-Boúúaert, "De Vicarii Substituti Constitutione ac Munere" —*Jus Pontificium,* VII (1927), 76, ad 2 (hereafter this article will be cited *De Vicario Substituto*).

A solution of the problem is not too difficult to find. Even though the cause of his absence was known beforehand, it completely slipped the pastor's mind, and consequently when the cause is brought to his attention again it becomes, as it were, something new and unexpected. Therefore the pastor could certainly make use of this canon to secure the services of a substitute vicar.[33]

The same solution would hold even though the cause of his absence had been overlooked through sheer negligence.[34]

C. Appeal to Rome

The third set of circumstances that demands the appointment of a substitute vicar is given in canon 1923, § 2.

> *Ad exsecutionem privationis beneficii iudex ne procedat contra clericum qui Sanctam Sedem adierit; sed si agatur de beneficio, cui adnexa sit animarum cura, Ordinarius provideat per designationem vicarii substituti.*

When a beneficiary appeals to Rome against a judicial sentence which deprives him of a benefice to which is attached the care of souls, the execution of the sentence cannot be carried out by the judge. But in order to safeguard the care of souls during the time of the pending appeal, the ordinary himself must designate a substitute vicar to take the place of the pastor until Rome has settled the matter.[35]

It must be remembered that the ordinary is obliged to appoint a substitute vicar only in the case of an appeal

---

33 Cf. Claeys-Boúúaert, "De Vicario Substituto"—*Jus Pontificium,* VII (1927), 76 ff.

34 Cf. Claeys-Boúúaert, *loc. cit.*

35 Cf. Claeys-Boúúaert, "De Vicario Substituto"—*Jus Pontificium,* VII (1927), 75; Cappello, "De Vicario Substituto"—*Periodica,* XIX (1930), 1*ff.; Vermeersch-Creusen, *Epitome,* I, n. 565.

from a judicial sentence. When there is question of recourse against an administrative decree of removal, the ordinary is free to appoint an administrator (*vicarius oeconomus*), and he does not select a substitute vicar to care for the spiritual needs of the parish.[36]

D. Absence of Less than a Week

The fourth case in which it is necessary for the pastor to have another take his place in the parish is indicated in canon 465, § 6.

> *Etiam pro tempore brevioris absentiae parochus debet fidelium necessitatibus providere, maxime si id peculiaria rerum adiuncta postulent.*

It is immediately evident that the priest who is supplying for the pastor is not a substitute vicar, since the pastor is not absent *ultra hebdomadam*.[37] It must be noted likewise that the pastor is not always obligated to select another priest to take his place when the absence from the parish is to be of a short duration. Such an appointment is obligatory only when the necessity of the faithful demands it.[38]

An example of such a necessity would be the presence of some very sick people in the parish, or a dangerous epidemic in the vicinity, or even the needed celebration of Mass on a special feast day.[39] As Fanfani indicates,[40] the care of

---

36 Vermeersch-Creusen, *Epitome,* I, n. 565; *Cappello,* "De Vicario Substituto"—*Periodica,* XIX (1930), 1*ff; Meier, *Penal Administrative Procedure Against Negligent Pastors,* The Catholic University of America Canon Law Studies, n. 140 (Washington, D.C.: The Catholic University of America Press, 1941), pp. 197-213, but especially 205 ff.

37 Cf. can. 465, §§ 4, 5; Cappello, "De Vicario Substituto"—*Periodica,* XIX (1930), 1*, ad 3; *infra,* p. 34, fn. 59.

38 Can. 465, § 6.

39 Cf. Ayrinhac, *Constitution of the Church,* n. 278, ad d.

40 *De Iure Parochorum* (Taurini, Romae: Marietti, 1924), n. 132, ad B.

souls can be given its needed attention, in an ordinary case, by a neighboring priest. This is true especially in a city where there are many parishes.[41] In a country parish, however, it is often necessary to call in another priest, since the nearest priest-neighbor may be many miles away.[42]

ARTICLE 3. JURIDICAL STATUS OF THE APPOINTEE

It is necessary at this point to determine the juridic status of the substitute vicar and of the supplying priest after they have received their appointment. For a clear understanding of their position in law it is imperative to know whether or not these clerics hold an ecclesiastical office. Once this point is settled, it will be relatively easy to determine the powers and faculties that they have.

The teaching of the pre-Code canonists regarding the nature of an ecclesiastical office was crystallized by Wernz in his standard definition: ". . . [officium est] gradus quidem iurisdictionis ecclesiasticae quoad personas, causas, locum, legibus Christi vel Ecclesiae in perpetuum ita institutus, ut iura et onera spiritualia ipsi adnexa nomine proprio et ratione quadam stabili sint exercenda." [43]

Thus it is evident that prior to 1918 the objective signification of an "ecclesiastical office" pointed to a certain measure or degree of jurisdiction as possessed by some ecclesiastical person in his appointment and as exercised by him in a fixed manner according to a permanent arrangement. Even at that time, however, there existed positions in the Church which were known as offices, but which did not imply for their incumbents the possession of strict jurisdictional power. At most, these offices consisted in the

---

41 Cf. Vermeersch-Creusen, *Epitome,* I, n. 553, ad 2º; Ayrinhac, *Constitution of the Church,* n. 258, ad d.

42 Cf. Fanfani, *De Iure Parochorum, loc. cit.;* Vermeersch-Creusen, *Epitome,* I, *loc. cit.*

43 *Ius Decretalium,* II, n. 240, ad 2.

administration of ecclesiastical things, such as the "offices" of *oeconomus*, sacristan, and the like.[44]

With the promulgation of the Code the essential notion of an ecclesiastical office did not undergo any change. But, by definition, an ecclesiastical office now can be thought of in two ways, namely, in a broad sense and in a strict sense.

In a broad sense an ecclesiastical office is defined as "*quodlibet munus quod in spiritualem finem legitime exercetur.*"[45] Thus it logically follows that neither the power of orders nor the power of jurisdiction is postulated as inherent in such an office. Consequently even lay persons may hold an ecclesiastical office if its concept be accepted in the broad sense.[46] Examples of such offices are found throughout the Code. Such offices are held, for instance, by superioresses of women religious,[47] by notaries,[48] and by judicial messengers and court bailiffs.[49]

In the strict sense, however, an ecclesiastical office is defined as a . . . *munus ordinatione sive divina sive ecclesiatica stabiliter constitutum, ad normam sacrorum canonum conferendum, aliquam saltem secumferens participationem ecclesiasticae potestatis sive ordinis sive iurisdictionis.*[50]

[44] Cf. c. un., X, *de officio primicerii*, I, 25; c. un., X, *de officio sacristae*, I, 26; Wernz, *Ius Decretalium*, II, n. 767, ad III; cc. 15, 41, *de praebendis et dignitatibus*, III, 4, in VI°; Ojetti, *Synopsis*, ad v. *officium*.

[45] Can. 145, § 1.

[46] Cf. Coronata, *Institutiones Iuris Canonici* (5 vols., Vol. I, ed. altera, Taurini: Marietti, 1939), I, 239 (hereafter cited *Institutiones*.)

[47] Cf. cans. 504; 529; 543; 2412; 2414.

[48] Cf. cans. 374, § 1 and 1585, § 2.

[49] Cf. can. 1591, §§ 1, 2. For other offices in the broad sense cf. Coronata, *Institutiones, loc. cit.*; Vermeersch-Creusen, *Epitome*, I, n. 263.

[50] Can. 145, § 1.

Thus an ecclesiastical office is an assignment which is to be entrusted to someone. As Coronata explains it,[51] an ecclesiastical office denotes the collection of rights and obligations which have been established with stability, that is, with objective perpetuity. The rights and the duties of the office must be established either by divine or ecclesiastical ordinance, and in such a manner that they always accompany an appointment or assignment that is made in accordance with the canonical norms. Such an appointment or assignment brings with it automatically a participation in that ecclesiatical power, either of orders or of jurisdiction, which inheres in the office authoritatively established.

When canon 145, § 1, mentions that stability is postulated for the existence of an office, it does not intend to imply that the office must always have an actual incumbent. It is requisite and sufficient that the fixed rights and obligations be transferred *ipso iure* to the one who is made the incumbent of the office. Therefore, an actual and continuous incumbency is not essential to the objective existence of an ecclesiastical office. The essential element is that the one appointed or assigned to the office participates in the power of orders or of jurisdiction that is attached to the office by means of a permanent provision.[52]

The general principles which determine whether or not a particular task or charge (*munus*) entrusted to a cleric is to be considered as an ecclesiastical office are clear. But, as Coronata points out, it is at times difficult to determine in a particular case whether there is question of an ecclesiastical office in the broad sense or in the strict sense.[53]

---

[51] *Institutiones*, I, 239 ff.

[52] Vermeersch-Creusen, *Epitome*, I, n. 263; Coronata, *Institutiones*, I, 239 ff.; Wernz-Vidal, *Ius Canonicum*, II, n. 140.

[53] *Institutiones*, I, *loc. cit.*

A. The Substitute Vicar

This difficulty seems to be present when there is discussion concerning the office of the substitute vicar. Are the powers of the substitute vicar granted to him by law, or does he receive them through a personal delegation? This difficulty can be solved by a careful consideration of the words of the text: "*Vicarius substitutus . . . locum parochi tenet in omnibus quae ad curam animarum spectant, nisi Ordinarius loci vel parochus aliquid exceperint.*"[54]

It appears from these words that the powers which are entrusted to the substitute are *ipso iure* connected with the position that he holds. When a substitute is legitimately appointed, it is not necessary for the pastor or the local ordinary to indicate the scope of his authority and powers or to grant him delegation in order to enable him to carry out the work entrusted to him. All that is taken care of by the law itself, which clearly indicates the limits of his powers and shares with him the necessary faculties.[55]

While it is true that the incumbency in the office of a substitute vicar is only a temporary one, such an incumbency is nevertheless accompanied with all the elements that are necessary to constitute, for the possessor, an ecclesiastical office in the strict sense. As a position which by law guarantees a certified possession of power, it is permanently established in the Church,[56] it is validly conferred if the various provisions of the canons are observed,[57] and it has attached to it all the powers of the pastor in regard to the care of souls as long as the local ordinary or

---

[54] Can. 474.

[55] Cf. Stocchiero, "De Jurisdictione Vicariorum Paroecialium"— *Jus Pontificium,* XI (1931), 148.

[56] Cf. cans. 474; 465, §§ 4, 5; 1923, § 2.

[57] Cf. *Pontificia Commissio Interpretationis* (P.C.I.), 14 iul. 1922—*Acta Apostolicae Sedis* (*AAS*), XIV (1922), 528.

the pastor has not specifically set any limitation.[58] Therefore, according to canon 197, § 1,[59] the power of the substitute vicar is an ordinary power.[60]

Most of the authors do not specifically state that the substitute vicar holds an ecclesiastical office. But that fact can be deduced from the words which they use. Vermeersch-Creusen,[61] for instance, state that the substitute vicar has ordinary jurisdiction to hear the confessions of the parishioners, to assist at their marriages, and the like. Since ordinary jurisdiction is that which is by law attached to an office,[62] it must be inferred that Vermeersch-Creusen believe that the substitute vicar has an ecclesiastical office in a proper and strict sense.[63]

If it should happen, however, that the pastor or the local ordinary restricts the power of the substitute vicar, is that to be taken as an indication for that particular case that the position is not to be regarded as an ecclesiastical office in the strict sense? Certainly not, for even though the pastor or the ordinary excepts something, the power which the substitute retains does not cease to be ordinary power, since it has been shared with him *ipso iure* once he is legitimately appointed.

---

58 Cans. 474 and 452, § 2. Cf. McBride, *Incardination and Excardination of Seculars,* The Catholic University of America Canon Law Studies, no. 145 (Washington, D.C.: The Catholic University of America Press 1941). pp. 484-485.

59 "Potestas iurisdictionis ordinaria ea est quae ipso iure adnexa est officio; delegata quae commissa est persona."

60 Cf. Cappello, "De Vicario Substituto"—*Periodica,* XIX (1929) 2*ff.

61 *Epitome,* I, n. 566.

62 Can. 197. § 1.

63 Cf. Coronata, *Institutiones,* I, 593; De Meester, *Juris Canonici et Juris Canonico-civilis Compendium* (3 vols. in 4, Brugis, 1921-1928), II, n. 370 (hereafter cited *Compendium*); Fanfani, *De iure Parochorum,* n. 251; Beste, *Introductio,* ad c. 474; Ayrinhac, *Constitution of the Church,* p. 356.

As Cappello states,[64] just as the retained power of the vicar general remains ordinary power according to canon 368, § 1, even when the bishop reserves some cases to himself, so does the power of the substitute vicar remain ordinary power even when the ordinary or the pastor excepts some cases from his jurisdiction. Therefore, within the limits of his jurisdiction and according to the norms given in the canons, the substitute vicar can delegate another priest either for a certain case or for all cases (*ad universitatem negotiorum*).[65]

B. The Supplying Priest

The case of a supplying priest who comes to a parish in order to care for the needs of the faithful during a brief absence of the pastor offers little difficulty. All authors agree that the supplying priest does not hold an ecclesiastical office in the strict and proper sense, since the powers which he possesses are not directly shared with him as deriving from the law itself.[66]

The authors, however, do dispute about the nature of the power possessed by the supplying priest. Vermeersch-Creusen, for example, contend that the supplying priest receives absolutely no power *a iure*, and that all of his powers must be delegated to him by the local ordinary or by the pastor.[67] Cappello agrees with this in the main.

64 " De Vicario Substituto "—*Periodica,* XIX (1930), 3*.

65 Can. 199, § 1. Cf. Claeys-Boúúaert, " De Vicario Substituto "—*Jus Pontificium,* VII (1927) 79, ad V. Regarding the power of the substitute to delegate in a particular case see Chapters V and VI.

66 Can. 465, 6. Cf. Vermeersch-Creusen, *Epitome,* I, n. 565; Cappello, " De Vicario Substituto "—*Periodica,* XIX (1930), 6*; Coronata, *Institutiones,* I, 585, footnote 1; Beste, *Introductio,* ad can. 474; Chelodi, *Ius de Personis* (ed. altera a Bertagnolli recognita et aucta, Tridenti: Ardesi, 1927) n. 229.

67 *Epitome,* I, n. 565. Cf. also Chelodi, *Ius de Personis,* n. 229, c, footnote 3.

He asserts that the supplying priest does not have ordinary power, nor a power that is delegated *a iure,* and that the supplying priest receives only those powers which the ordinary or the pastor delegates to him. He further states, however, that this delegation is to be assumed as given with the authorization to administer all pastoral matters unless an exception is made by the one who delegates the supplying priest.[68]

Coronata states that the supplying priest may be delegated with power that extends to all the matters of pastoral care, and that such a comprehensive delegation will include also the power to assist at matrimony.[69] He reasons that the good of souls demands such a universal delegation. He admits that the supplying priest is neither an assistant in the sense contemplated in canon 1096, § 1, nor a substitute in the sense implied in canon 474. Nevertheless he claims that the supplying priest is a substitute *de facto,* and therefore he can be regarded as having by express delegation the same powers that the real substitute has by law.

The question of the supplying priest's power to assist at marriages will be more fully treated in Chapter VII. It is sufficient here to indicate that Coronata's reasoning seems specious and directly contrary to the law enacted in canon 1096, wherein it is expressly stated that a general delegation to assist at marriages cannot be given except to parochial assistants. Since the law there makes no further distinctions or exceptions, it does not appear permissible to extend the meaning of the words of that canon to include cases other than those expressly mentioned.[70]

---

68 "De Vicario Substituto"—*Periodica,* XIX (1930), 6*.

69 *Institutiones,* I, 585, footnote 1.

70 Cf. can 18.

It may be concluded, then, that if the supplying priest is given a general delegation by the pastor to provide for the care of souls during the latter's absence, the supplying priest receives a power which in its fullness and comprehensiveness is limited only in so far as the law indicates definite restrictions.[71] If the supplying priest receives only certain specified powers from the pastor, then he must remain within the limits of the mandate he has received.

---

[71] Thus the pastor could not grant delegation to hear confessions, for according to the norms of canon 874 that power cannot be delegated by the pastor.

CHAPTER II

Appointment

The Council of Trent [1] decreed that bishops were obliged "*providere, ut per deputationem idoneorum vicariorum . . . cura animarum nullatenus negligatur.*" The obligation of securing the services of such a substitute, however, rested upon the pastor, as can be seen from the decision of the same Council: "*. . . quandocumque eos* [*i.e. parochos*], *causa prius per episcopum cognita et probata, abesse contigerit, vicarium idoneum, ab ipso Ordinario approbandum . . . relinquant.*" [2]

Thus the Council of Trent, while insisting on the obligation of having someone present at the parish to take care of the needs of the faithful, did not specify what length of absence on the part of the pastor made it mandatory for him to secure the services of a vicar, or what powers such a vicar had once he was appointed.

The Sacred Congregation of the Council, while giving several decisions relating to these vicars, contented itself with reiterating the general principles enacted by the Council of Trent.[3] This Congregation, however, did coin the word "*vicarius substitutus*", which has been adopted by the present Code.[4]

---

[1] Sess. XXIII, *de ref.*, c.l.

[2] Sess. XXIII, *loc cit.*

[3] S.C.C., *Fulginaten.*, 10 maii 1687, ad 1; S.C.C., *Vicen.*, 7 oct. 1604—*Codicis Iuris Canonici Fontes* cura Emi. Petri Card. Gasparri Editi (9 vols., Romae [postea Civitate Vaticana]: Typis Polyglottis Vaticanis, 1923-1939, [Vols. VII, VIII et IX ed. cura et studio Emi. Iustiniani Card. Serédi]), n. 2899; n. 2352 (hereafter cited *Fontes*).

[4] S.C.C., *Vicen.*, 7 oct. 1604—*Fontes*, n. 2352.

Since May 19, 1918, when the present Code became binding law, the method of appointing a priest to take the place of an absent pastor has been definitely established. The purpose of the following articles will be to investigate the various ways in which this appointment may be made.

ARTICLE 1. NOMINATION OF A SUBSTITUTE VICAR

A. Who May Make the Nomination?

In an ordinary case the appointment of a substitute vicar is divided into two separate and distinct phases—the nomination by the pastor and the approbation by the local ordinary.[5] There exists one set of circumstances, however in which the pastor is obliged to forego his right of appointing a substitute. This case is mentioned in canon 1923, § 2: "*Ad exsecutionem privationis beneficii iudex ne procedat contra clerum qui Sanctam Sedem adierit; sed si agatur de beneficio, cui adnexa sit animarum cura, Ordinarius provideat per designationem vicarii substituti.*"

The authors agree [6] that under such circumstances the bishop alone has the right to provide for the care of souls in the parish. It is the bishop, therefore, who has the right to appoint a substitute vicar who will hold office until the Holy See has decided the case.

It may sometimes happen that the pastor who is making the appeal will suggest as a substitute a priest who has all the necessary qualifications. Even in such a case the bishop is not obliged to follow the pastor's suggestion. And should it happen that the bishop's appointment of some particular substitute prove displeasing to the pastor, the latter has no

---

[5] Cf. can. 465, §§ 4, 5.

[6] Cf. Cappello, "De Vicario Substituto"—*Periodica,* XIX (1930), 1*, n. 2; Claeys-Boúúaert, "De Vicario Substituto"—*Jus Pontificium,* VII (1927), 78, n. 5; Chelodi, *Ius de Personis,* n. 229; Coronata, *Institutiones,* I, 593.

legal redress against the appointment as long as the substitute properly fulfills his duties.

The regular method of appointment, however, consists in the nomination by the pastor and the subsequent approbation by the bishop. The law specifies[7] that whenever a pastor is to be absent from his parish for over seven continuous days he is obliged to secure the services of a substitute vicar. This substitute has charge of the parish in all matters which pertain to the care of souls.[8]

The reason why the pastor is to be absent does not enter into the question, since the law makes no distinction between one kind of absence and another. So, whether a pastor is absent over a week on his vacation, or whether he is absent because of sickness, he is obliged to secure a substitute who takes his place.

The pastor's presentation of the vicar to the ordinary for approbation is not new legislation. Pre-Code authors[9] almost unanimously agreed that it was the duty of the one who had the care of souls to secure his own vicar during his absence. The only exception made in present day legislation is the one indicated at the beginning of this chapter.[10]

B. Who May Receive the Nomination?

After a pastor discovers that he will be absent from his parish for over a week, he must secure the services of a substitute. But, before he can do that, he must be able to

---

7 Can. 465, §§ 4, 5.

8 Cf. Cappello, "De Vicario Substituto"—*Periodica,* XIX (1930), 1*.

9 Cf. Ferraris, *Bibliotheca,* ad v. *vicarius parochialis,* n. 48; Pirhing, *Jus Canonicum,* Lib. I, tit. 28, n. 21; Reiffenstuel, *Jus Canonicum,* Lib. I, tit. 28, n. 52; Barbosa, *Collectanea Doctorum in Ius Pontificium* (Lugduni: 1632) Lib. III, c. 6, n. 63.

10 The exception referred to is that of a priest who appeals to Rome from a judicial sentence of removal from a benefice to which is attached the care of souls.

answer the question: who may be chosen as a substitute? The Code itself does not specify the qualities that the vicar must possess, but it does demand that the substitute be approved by the ordinary of the place.[11] The pastor, therefore, must choose a priest who can receive the approval of the bishop.

If the pastor desires his substitute to possess special qualities and qualifications because of the special conditions that exist in his parish, the pastor must himself find and secure the services of this specially qualified priest.

Should it happen that the pastor has one or more assistants, he may choose one of them as his vicar during the time of his absence, unless some particular law specifies otherwise.[12] Claeys-Boúúaert contends [13] that there is no regulation in the universal law of the Church that would prevent a neighboring pastor from being named as substitute vicar during the absence of the proper pastor. This, however, does not seem to be universally true. The primary concern of the pastor as well as of the substitute is the proper care of souls. From the earliest times the Church has insisted upon personal residence by the pastor in order to safeguard the rights of the faithful to a suitable and personal pastoral care.[14] Consequently it seems that it is incompatible for one and the same priest to be the pastor in one parish and at the same time the substitute vicar in another. Such an arrangement seems to be contrary to the law of personal residence.[15]

Nevertheless, if there exists a just and proportionate

---

[11] Can. 465, §§ 4, 5. Cf. Section C of this chapter.

[12] Cf. Claeys-Boúúaert, "De Vicario Substituto"—*Jus Pontificium,* VII (1927), 78, ad IV.

[13] "De Vicario Substituto," *loc. cit.*

[14] Cf. Chap. I, p. 3.

[15] Can. 461, § 1.

cause, it is probably within the power of the local ordinary to grant a dispensation [16] whereby he permits such an arrangement, just as he can permit a pastor to live outside his parish for a just cause.[17] In all cases, however, the rights of the parishioners to a proper service must be safeguarded.[18]

A further question which must be decided is whether a pastor, on his own authority, may choose a priest from another diocese to act as his vicar. It may happen that a pastor whose parish borders on another diocese, or for other reasons, may find it more convenient to secure the services of a substitute from the neighboring diocese than from his own. May the pastor present to the bishop for approval a priest who does not possess faculties in the diocese where he is to act as substitute?

Viewed solely from the standpoint of the present Code, the answer must be in the affirmative. Canon 465, §§ 4, 5, does not limit the pastor's power to the *presenting of a priest from his own diocese.* The bishop, however, may refuse to approve such a priest. In such a case the pastor will be compelled to nominate another as substitute.[19]

C. *Needed Approval for the Nomination.*

After the pastor has nominated the priest whom he wants to act as his substitute, the approval of the ordinary must intervene before the priest is validly appointed as sub-

---

16 Cf. can. 81.

17 Can. 465, § 1.

18 Can. 465, § 1. Claeys-Boúúaert ("De Vicario Substituto"—*Jus Pontificium, loc. cit.*) admits the difficulty of serving two churches at the same time: "Si eligatur parochus vicinus, cavendum est ne difficilis sit paroeciarum ad invicem accessus et ne, propter utriusque curae onera, alterutrum munus quasi necessario negligatur."

19 Cf. Claeys-Boúúaert, "De Vicario Substituto"—*Jus Pontificium,* VII (1927), 78, ad IV.

stitute vicar.[20] The Code also demands, in the case of a religious pastor, the consent of the religious superior.[21] The discussion of these two points will constitute the subject matter for this section.

1. The Needed Approval of the Local Ordinary.

Most authors agree that the approval of the local ordinary is required for the valid appointment of a substitute vicar in every foreseen absence of more than one week.[22] This general agreement stems from a decision handed down by the Pontifical Commission for the Interpretation of the Code. The Commission was asked:

1. Whether the vicar substitute spoken of in c. 465, § 4, can, after the approval of the Ordinary, licitly and validly assist at marriages if no limitation was imposed.

Reply. In the affirmative.

2. Whether the same vicar can do so before the Ordinary's approval.

Reply. In the negative.[23] It seems evident, therefore, that it is the approval of the ordinary that constitutes the priest as the legitimate substitute vicar. This approval should be given in writing, but a written approval is not required for the validity of the bishop's act.[24]

---

[20] Can. 465, § 4. An exception to this rule is the appointment of a substitute by the pastor in an urgent case. This case will be considered in Section E of this chapter.

[21] Can. 465, §§ 4, 5.

[22] Cf. Claeys-Boúúaert, "De Vicario Substituto"—*Jus Pontificium,* VII (1927), 76; Cappello, "De Vicario Substituto"— *Periodica,* XIX (1930), 4*; Vermeersch-Creusen, *Epitome,* I, n. 565. The case of a pastor who does not secure the prior approbation of the ordinary because of inadvertence, forgetfulness and the like, will be treated under Section D of this chapter.

[23] Bouscaren, *Canon Law Digest* (2 vols., Milwaukee: Bruce Publishing Co., 1934-1943) I, can. 1095; *AAS,* XIV (1922), 528.

[24] Cf. can. 11; Claeys-Boúúaert, "De Vicario Substituto"— *Jus Pontificium,* VII (1927), 77.

The canons do not determine just how this approval is to be specified. Must the approbation of the ordinary be explicit and determined in each case, or will an implicit and indeterminate approbation suffice? Is it possible for the ordinary to concede faculties to a pastor so that any time he is to be absent for over a week he is permitted to secure the services of, for instance, any religious of a particular house who is sent by the superior?

From the standpoint of the general law there does not seem to be any reason why this cannot be done. It appears to constitute a legitimate designation of a substitute.[25] As Cappello indicates,[26] the bishop is giving a true approbation, not indeed to a particular religious by name, but in general to all the religious of a particular house. When the superior actually sends a priest religious to take the place of the absent pastor, the religious who is sent is by that very fact specifically approved.

Claeys-Boúúaert, on the other hand, seems to disagree with this solution.[27] He asserts that the wording of canon 465, § 5, demands a formal and express designation in each case. But he admits that the cause of the absence does not have to be verified before, or even simultaneously with, the petition which, when sent to the ordinary, asks for the approval of a particular substitute. Nor is it necessary to seek a special approval in each individual case. It is sufficient for the pastor to secure beforehand the bishop's approval of a particular priest who is to take charge of the parish whenever an absence of over a week occurs.

From this it is evident that fundamentally the two authors are not in disagreement. Claeys-Boúúaert[28] can-

---

[25] Cf. Vermeersch-Creusen, *Epitome*, I, 565.

[26] "De Vicario Substituto"—*Periodica*, XIX (1930), 3*, ad 6.

[27] "De Vicario Substituto"—*Jus Pontificium*, VII (1927), 77.

[28] "De Vicario Substituto," *loc. cit.*

not conceive of valid episcopal approval being given to any unspecified priest, as, for example, to any neighboring priest who would be willing to accept the position of substitute during the pastor's absence. Cappello [29] agrees with this. In the example of the pastor calling a priest from a particular house, Cappello does not assert that an indiscriminate approbation is permissible. He merely claims that all the priests of the house are approved in general, so that when an individual priest is sent by the superior the approval of the ordinary becomes particularized in that case.

Since it is within the power of the superior to send any of his subjects to take the place of the pastor, there is no reason why, according to the case given above, he could not recall the priest whom he has sent originally in order to have another of his subjects take the pastor's place.[30]

At this point it is necessary to discuss the status of the vicar if the ordinary withdraws his approval. It has already been pointed out that the approbation of the bishop is necessary for the validity of the appointment in a foreseen absence of over a week.[31] Therefore the substitute, after notification of the withdrawal of approbation, can no longer be considered as the legitimate substitute vicar.[32]

If the priest who had been originally selected by the pastor possessed the faculties of the diocese, for instance, to hear confessions and to preach, such faculties can still be validly and lawfully used. The pastor may also give this priest specific delegation to perform other functions. But

---

29 " De Vicario Substituto," *loc. cit.*

30 Cf. Cappello, " De Vicario Substituto," *loc. cit.*

31 Cf. first part of this section.

32 Cf. Claeys-Boúúaert, " De Vicario Substituto "—*Jus Pontificium,* VII (1927), 76.

without episcopal approval the priest cannot be considered as a substitute vicar in the strict canonical sense.[33]

2. The Requisite Approval of the Religious Superior.

Besides the approbation of the local ordinary, the Code demands that when a religious pastor absents himself for over a week, the superior of the pastor must also approve the substitute who is to be appointed.[34] This permission is called for even though the parish is not united "*pleno iure*" to the religious institute, as when [35] the parish is placed in the temporary charge of a pastor who is a religious.[36]

The consent of the religious superior is required by the law in view of the bond of obedience that exists between the pastor and his superior, and because of the special relation that is created between the pastor and his substitute.[37]

The required consent of the superior is, however, not demanded for the validity of the appointment. This is admitted by all the authors.[38] They base their opinion on a response given by the Pontifical Commission for the Interpretation of the Code. This Commission was asked whether the substitute vicar spoken of in can. 465, § 5, could validly and lawfully assist at marriages after the approval of the ordinary but before the approval of the re-

---

34 Can. 465, § 4.

35 Cf. can. 1425, § 2.

36 Cf. Claeys-Boúúaert, "De Vicario Substituto"—*Jus Pontificium,* VII (1927), 77 ff.

37 Cf. Claeys-Boúúaert "De Vicario Substituto," *loc. cit.*

38 Cf. Cappello, "De Vicario Substituto"—*Periodica,* XIX (1930), 4*; Claeys-Boúúaert, "De Vicario Substituto"—*Jus Pontificium,* VII (1927), 77 ff.; Vermeersch-Creusen, *Epitome,* I, n. 565, ad 2.

33 Cf. Claeys-Boúúaert, "De Vicario Substituto," *loc. cit.*

ligious superior had been given. The reply given was in the affirmative.[39]

Therefore, if the religious pastor does not obtain the approval of his superior either because of forgetfulness, or perhaps through malice, or for any other reason, the appointment of the substitute is valid as long as the approval of the ordinary is had. In such an appointment the pastor has acted unlawfully inasmuch as he has not fulfilled all the law. But the acts of jurisdiction performed by the substitute will nevertheless be valid acts.

D. Nomination and Approval in a Foreseen Absence of Over a Week.

There are two sets of circumstances in which a pastor can know that he will be absent from his parish for over a week. Thus he may be voluntarily absent, as, for instance, to spend a vacation or to undergo a previously planned operation, or he may be involuntarily absent, as, for instance, when he has appealed to Rome from a judicial sentence of removal from his parish, and the ordinary has appointed a substitute to govern the parish during the time of the pending appeal.

1. Voluntary Absence of Over a Week.

Any pastor who knows beforehand that he will be absent from his parish for over a week must obtain a written permission from the ordinary, and the substitute whom the pastor selects must thereupon be approved by the ordinary.[40] The substitute thus appointed takes the place of the pastor in all things that pertain to the care of souls.[41]

---

[39] " 3. Utrum idem vicarius [substitutus] parochi religiosi [de quo in can. 465, § 4,] id possit [i.e. licite et valide assistere matrimoniis] post approbationem Ordinarii, sed ante approbationem Superioris religiosi. Resp. ad 3. Affirmative."—*AAS,* XIV (1922), 527-528, ad V, n. 3.

[40] Can. 465, § 4. Cf. *supra* pp. 24 ff.

[41] Can. 474.

If the ordinary refuses to approve a particular priest or a particular group of priests, for example, priests from outside the diocese, then another priest must be presented by the pastor until the bishop does give his approval.[42]

Although the theory is very exact and definite, it is possible that difficulties may arise in a practical case. For example, a pastor knows two weeks in advance that he will have to undergo an operation that will incapacitate him for about ten days. In due time he writes to the ordinary and asks him to approve Fr. X as substitute. This letter, as occasionally happens, is lost in the mail.

On the day when the pastor is supposed to leave for the hospital he remembers that the man he proposed as his substitute vicar has not yet received approbation from the bishop. Now he wonders whether he may call upon Fr. X to take charge of the parish, and what powers Fr. X will possess if he does take charge?

Claeys-Boúúaert writes[43] that according to the strict text of the Code the designation of the pastor would seem to be valid. He reasons that the first consideration of the Code is the actual appointment of a vicar to care for the needs of the parishioners. The power to designate the substitute rests solely on the pastor; the ordinary merely approves or disapproves the pastor's choice.

But, as Claeys-Boúúaert also points out, the text has taken on a restricted meaning from a response given by the Pontifical Commission. This Commission was asked whether the substitute vicar, spoken of in can. 465, § 4, could validly and lawfully assist at marriages even before the approval that is to be given by the ordinary. The given response was in the negative.[44] It can be concluded, then,

[42] Cf. Claeys-Boúúaert, "De Vicario Substituto"—*Jus Pontificium,* VII (1927), 78, ad IV.

[43] "De Vicario Substituto"—*Jus Pontificium,* VII (1927), 75 ad III.

[44] P.C.I., 14 iul. 1922 ad V—*AAS,* XIV (1922), 527-528.

that at least in every non-urgent case the valid appointment of the substitute depends on the will and approval of the bishop.[45] Therefore, if the pastor does not present a priest for approval, or if the pastor does not receive notification that the approval has been given, the presumption is that the priest selected by the pastor does not possess, as such, the special faculties of a substitute vicar.

One must not immediately conclude that the pastor will have to postpone his operation until some later day. In practice a different solution, one that is in conformity with the text of the Code and the decision of the Pontifical Commission, can be found.

If the approbation of the ordinary does not arrive in time, or even if the pastor did not ask the bishop to approve a certain priest, and the cause of the absence is truly grave and urgent, the faculty given to the pastor in can. 465, § 5, may be used.[46] Cappello agrees with this solution.[47] He proposes that the ruling of canon 465, § 5, becomes applicable also when the pastor has forgotten to notify the bishop regarding his foreseen absence.

This opinion seems to be in accordance with the wording of the law. It appears perfectly lawful to follow the

[45] Cf. Claeys-Boúúaert, "De Vicario Substituto," *loc. cit.*

[46] Urgent cases of absence will be treated in more detail in Section E of this chapter. Cf. Claeys-Boúúaert, "De Vicario Substituto," *loc cit.*

[47] "De Vicario Substituto"—*Periodica,* XIX (1930), 5*ff. Vermeersch-Creusen (*Epitome,* I, n. 565, footnote 2) seem to disagree, stating that the arguments appear not to be cogent. It seems, however, that Vermeersch-Creusen base their argument on can. 465, § 4, and on the reply of the Pontifical Commission as given on July 14, 1922, wherein it is made evident that the approbation of the local ordinary is necessary for the validity of the appointment in every *foreseen* absence of over a week. Claeys-Boúúaert and Cappello do not disagree with this. They merely declare that if the pastor's unpostponable absence had developed as a grave and urgent need, then the pastor may make use of the alternative granted in can. 465, § 5, instead of the rule stated in can. 465, § 4.

opinion that, if the ordinary has not been asked to approve the substitute for any reason whatsoever, and the cause of the absence has actually become a grave and urgent one, then the pastor can make use of the powers given him in canon 465, § 5, and establish a substitute by his own authority.

The solution of the proposed case, then, is as follows: The pastor is certainly permitted to leave his parish in charge of Fr. X. Since the operation which must be undergone constitutes a grave and urgent reason for the pastor's absence, Fr. X has all the faculties of a substitute vicar.[48]

Another possible case can readily be visualized. The pastor does not definitely know whether he will be absent from his parish for over a week or for a shorter time only. Is he, nevertheless, obliged to secure the services of a substitute vicar?

If the doubt is of a positive and probable character, then the pastor is not obliged to designate a substitute, since a doubtful law involves no certain obligations.[49] The needs of the faithful can be taken care of in various other ways apart from the appointing of a substitute. For example, the pastor may make use of the services of his assistant, if he has one, or he may secure the services of a supplying priest,[50] or he may have a neighboring priest administer the more necessary sacraments during the time of his absence. In such cases of doubt, however, the diocesan statutes will usually enact pertinent regulations which are to be followed in each case.[51]

---

[48] For further details cf. Subdivision E of this chapter.

[49] Cf. can. 15; Claeys-Boúúaert, "De Vicario Substituto"—*Jus Pontificium,* VII (1927), 74.

[50] Cf. can. 465, § 6.

[51] Cf. Claeys-Boúúaert, "De Vicario Substituto," *loc. cit.*

2. Enforced Absence of Over a Week.

The only case given by the authors regarding a pastor's enforced absence is that of the pastor who, when he has been deprived of his parish by judicial sentence, appeals his case to Rome.[52]

After the trial has been brought to a close and the cleric has been found guilty, the judge may not proceed to the execution of the sentence of privation if the cleric has made an appeal to Rome. Since the original pastor may not return to his parish to administer to the needs of the faithful lest scandal be given or bewilderment ensue among the parishioners, the ordinary himself must provide for the parishioners by designating a priest who will act as substitute vicar until Rome has decided the case.[53]

E. Nomination and Approval in a Case of Urgent Absence.

1. The Nomination by the Pastor.

Canon 465, § 5, indicates the manner in which a substitute vicar is to be constituted in a case of urgent absence. The pastor who is to be absent for over a week in consequence of some grave cause which has unexpectedly arisen is obliged to communicate with his ordinary to indicate the the reason for his absence, but will at the same time name the priest who is to take his place.[54]

The two postulated conditions that must be verified on the part of the pastor are: 1) the cause of the absence must

---

52 Cf. can. 474; 1923, § 2; Claeys-Boúúaert, " De Vicario Substituto "—*Jus Pontificium,* VII (1927), 78; Cappello, " De Vicario Substituto "—*Periodica,* XIX (1930), 1*; Vermeersch-Creusen, *Epitome,* I, n. 565; Coronata, *Institutiones,* I, 593.

53 Cf. *supra,* p. 20.

54 Can. 465, § 5, speaks of the *"sacerdos supplens."* But that such a priest is a substitute vicar is indicated in can. 474: " Vicarius substitutus qui constituitur ad norman can. 465, §§ 4, 5 . . . locum parochi tenet . . ."

be an unexpected one that is truly urgent, and 2) the pastor's absence must be one which needs to be protracted for more than a week.[55] There is no question of securing the previous permission of the ordinary; the cause of the pastor's absence is urgent and cannot brook any delay.[56] Immediately upon the act of designation by the pastor the priest chosen receives and enjoys the full office of substitute vicar.

Just how is the element of unexpectedness to be interpreted? If the urgency of the case or the gravity of the cause are of a purely subjective character, without any objective basis, is the pastor's designation of the vicar made validly?

Certainly canon 465, § 5, was inserted into the Code with a view to safeguarding primarily the rights of the faithful regarding the needed spiritual care.[57] And it seems just as evident that the pastor must make a decision, carefully weighing the relative merits and circumstances of each individual case. If he decides that the case at hand is truly urgent and grave, he may safely leave his parish in the hands of a substitute vicar. If the pastor's judgment is erroneous, so that his reasons for going away are objectively not actually urgent or grave, the appointment would nevertheless be valid, and the acts of jurisdiction performed by the substitute would likewise be valid.[58]

[55] It has been demonstrated in Art. 1, subdivision D, of this chapter that as long as these two conditions are present, even if they are the result of the pastor's own negligence, the alternative granted by can. 465, § 5, may be used.

[56] Cf. Claeys-Boúúaert, "De Vicario Substituto"—*Jus Pontificium,* VII (1927), 76 ff.

[57] Cf. Claeys-Boúúaert, "De Vicario Substituto," *loc. cit.;* Coronata, *Institutiones,* I, 584, footnote 4.

[58] Canon 209 would seem to have application here: . . . in dubio positivo et probabili sive iuris sive facti, iurisdictionem supplet Ecclesia pro foro tum externo tum interno. Cf. Coronata, *Institutiones,* I, *loc. cit.*

The second element which is postulated for the validity of the pastor's designation of the substitute is that the absence needs to be protracted for over a week.[59] In an evident case the application of this principle is clear, as, for example, in the case of an unexpected illness on the part of the pastor. Nevertheless one may point to three cases in which some difficulty in the application of the principle may arise.

The first case concerns the pastor who doubts whether his absence from the parish will be protracted for over a week. Considering the matter he finds weighty arguments both pro and con which preclude any definite and certain decision on his part. Just what is his obligation in such a case?

Claeys-Boúúaert claims[60] that the pastor is not obliged to appoint a substitute. As long as there exists a reasonable and positive doubt, it is probable that the pastor can permissibly appoint or also forego appointing a substitute, just as he sees fit.[61]

The second case is that of the pastor who expects to be gone for more than a week and accordingly secures the

---

[59] This seems to follow from a study of canon 474. This canon states that a substitute vicar, when he is appointed according to the norms of canons 465, §§ 4, 5, and canon 1923, § 2, takes the place of the pastor in all things that pertain to the care of souls, unless the local ordinary or the pastor excepts some duty from his care. Canon 474 apparently adverts to all the ways in which a substitute vicar may be appointed. Consequently, if the substitute must be appointed according to the norms of canons 465, §§ 4, 5, an absence of over a week is postulated, since both of the paragraphs in canon 465 specify an absence "*ultra hebdomadam.*" If the absence is not protracted over a week, then the norms are inapplicable, and consequently no question of the appointment of a substitute vicar really obtains in the case. Cf. can. 11. Cappello ("De Vicario Substituto," —*Periodica*, XIX 1930, 1*) agrees with this, for he states: "Ex dictis sponte manifesteque consequitur, vicarium substitutum non haberi in sequentibus casibus: 1º si parochi absentia a paroecia non sit ultra hebdomadam."

[60] "De Vicario Substituto"—*Jus Pontificium*, VII (1927), 74 ff.

[61] Cf. Section D of this chapter.

assistance of a substitute vicar. After several days, however, the pastor returns to his parish. Are the acts performed by the substitute during the pastor's absence of less than a week to be considered as valid acts?

The answer to this question must be an affirmative one. The pastor, before he left, was morally certain that he would be gone for more than a week. The appointment was therefore valid. A subsequent change in circumstances will not have retroactive force so as to render invalid the appointment which was validly made some days before.[62]

The third case concerns the pastor who believes that he will be absent from his parish for less than a week, but who in actuality remains away for more than seven days. How is one, upon the lapse of the seven days, to regard the status of the priest who was left in charge at the parish?

Cappello is of the opinion[63] that the supplying priest who was appointed by the pastor can, after the lapse of the seven days, legitimately exercise the care of souls and validly assist at marriages. Coronata's opinion appears to be even more liberal.[64] He contends not only that upon the lapse of the seven days does the supplying priest become the substitute vicar, but also that his earlier acts (e.g., assistance at marriage), even when placed in bad faith while the pastor was actually not yet absent for over a week, are also valid, apart altogether from the added consideration of common error, since in the given situation the pastor's absence can rightly be regarded as one which was necessitated *ultra hebdomadam.*

Both these authors seem to overlook the important point of " designation " by the pastor. A practical case may here

---

62 Cf. Cappello, " De Vicario Substituto "—*Periodica,* XIX (1930), 5*.

63 " De Vicario Substituto "—*Periodica,* XIX (1930), 5*.

64 *Institutiones,* I, 584, footnote 4.

be contemplated. A pastor leaves his parish to attend the sickbed of a parent. Since he expects to be absent for three or four days at the longest, he secures simply the services of a supplying priest. After an absence of several days the pastor himself becomes ill. No word is sent to the supplying priest that the pastor is ill. Likewise no notice is given to the supplying priest that he is to function as a substitute vicar. Can this priest, then, after the pastor is actually absent for over seven days, presuppose that he is automatically given the office of substitute vicar?

Such an inference appears to be out of order, for the bare minimum that is demanded by canon 465, § 5, has not been fulfilled: the priest was not appointed as a substitute by the pastor.

If the pastor had told the supplying priest that he should assume full charge of the parish in the event that the absence was protracted beyond seven days, then the supposition that he could become a substitute vicar would be in favor of the supplying priest. Without such a potential designation by the pastor it seems rather that the supplying priest could never consider himself as the substitute vicar even upon the lapse of the pastor's absence for a full week.

2. The Approbation by the Ordinary.

Canon 465, § 5, indicates that the ordinary is to be notified whenever the pastor finds it imperative to leave his parish in view of some grave and urgent reason. The letter of notification must explain the reason for the pastor's absence, and also give the name of the substitute vicar whom the pastor is leaving in his stead. The bishop may, if he sees fit, limit the powers of the substitute.

It is now necessary to determine whether or not the notification that is to be sent to the ordinary is a requirement which is essential for the validity of the pastor's act whereby the substitute is designated.

Claeys-Boúúaert proposes a solution [65] without definitely solving the difficulty. He claims that even though the pastor forgets to notify the ordinary, it is the mind of the legislator that the notification should be made even after he has left the parish. But if at the time of the notification the pastor's absence will not continue for seven more days, then there is no obligation on the pastor's part to constitute a substitute, since the Code supposes the absence to be protracted for the period of a week when it insists on the appointment of a substitute.

Cappello [66] hits closer to the heart of the problem. He states that if the ordinary was not notified, either because the letter was lost in the mail, or even because the pastor was negligent, then the appointment nevertheless remains valid. Coronata [67] agrees with this solution, offering as his reason the decision of the Pontifical Commission for the Interpretation of the Code, and also the good of souls which should not suffer because of the error or fault of the pastor.

The decision of the Pontifical Commission to which Coronata refers [68] was an answer to a question that had been proposed for solution. The Commission was asked whether the vicar spoken of in canon 465, § 5, could validly and lawfully assist at marriages before the approval of the ordinary. The answer was in the affirmative, but with the proviso and on the condition that the ordinary has left the previous arrangement intact and unaltered. Fanfani contends [69] that the priest spoken of in canon 465, § 5, does not become a true substitute vicar until he is accepted by the ordinary.

---

65 " De Vicario Substituto "—*Jus Pontificium,* VII, (1927), 74.

66 " De Vicario Substituto "—*Periodica,* XIX (1930), 5* ff.

67 *Institutiones,* I, 584, footnote 4.

68 P.C.I., 14 iul. 1922, ad V,—*AAS,* XIV (1922), 528.

69 *De Iure Parochorum,* n. 446.

The important point that must be kept in mind is that the primary consideration is the needs of the faithful. That seems evident from the Code itself,[70] and also from the decision of the Code Commission quoted above, where it is explicitly stated that the substitute receives authority from the moment he is designated by the pastor. From the same decision it is evident that the acts performed by the vicar before the ordinary receives the notification are likewise valid.[71] It seems, therefore, a safe opinion to hold that, even though the pastor does not notify the ordinary at all, the appointment of the substitute is valid, and the acts performed by the vicar are likewise valid.

If the bishop, however, learns of this, he is permitted to limit the power of the substitute, and even to demand that the pastor secure the services of a different priest. If the pastor refuses to obey the bishop, the ordinary himself is then empowered to remove the substitute and to put another in his place.[72]

ARTICLE 2. THE APPOINTMENT OF THE SUPPLYING PRIEST

The supplying priest who takes the place of the pastor during the latter's absence for less than a week does not have to be approved by the ordinary, according to the general law.[73] Since such a priest is to take the place of the pastor, it is the duty of the pastor himself to secure the services of the priest.

---

[70] Can. 465, § 5.

[71] Cf. Claeys-Boúúaert, "De Vicario Substituto"—*Jus Pontificium,* VII (1927), 77.

[72] Cf. Claeys-Boúúaert, "De Vicario Substituto," *loc cit.*: "Sequitur enim e proprio episcopi in totam dioecesim regimine neminem delegari posse, potissimum in universitatem causarum contra ipsius episcopi beneplacitum."

[73] Cf. Cappello, "De Vicario Substituto"—*Periodica,* XIX (1930), 6*. Particular law may, however, demand the episcopal approbation of the priest who renders the needed pastoral service even for the shorter absences of less than a week.

As far as the law of the Code is concerned, the pastor has a complete liberty of choice: he may secure the services of a priest who already possesses faculties within the diocese, or he may obtain the help of an extradiocesan priest. The supplying priest, however, unlike the substitute vicar, does not obtain any special faculties by virtue of his appointment. The only powers he has are the ones that are delegated to him by the pastor, but it is outside the competence of the pastor [74] to share with the supplying priest, by way of an act of delegation, his own pastoral jurisdiction for the hearing of sacramental confessions.[75]

[74] Cf. *supra*, p. 16; Coronata, *Institutiones*, I, 584-585; Cappello, "De Vicario Substituto," *loc. cit.;* Chelodi, *Ius de Personis*, n. 229, footnote 3.

[75] Cf. can. 874, § 1; P.C.I., 16 oct. 1919, ad 3—*AAS*, XI (1919), 477.

CHAPTER III

Scope and Extent of the Substitute's Office

In the pre-Code era the temporary vicar, like the substitute vicar, was appointed to serve a particular church for a certain period of time.[1] At the time of his appointment the temporary vicar received the jurisdiction necessary for him to perform both validly and lawfully certain parochial functions. Pirhing (1606-1679) called this jurisdiction "*veluti ordinaria,*"[2] since it was the same kind of jurisdiction that was possessed by the one whose place he was taking, for although the exercise of the jurisdiction was restricted to a certain length of time, it was not restricted to a particular set or number of acts.

Thus it followed that, although the temporary vicar did exercise the parochial care of souls, still the *right* to the parish and to the care of souls remained with the one whose place he was taking. The vicar merely exercised the rights, not as though they belonged to him, but in view of his commission and in the name of the one whose place he was taking.[3]

The same principles can be applied almost in their entirety to substitute vicars. A substitute vicar, when legitimately appointed[4] according to the norms of canon 474, is considered in law as possessing all the rights and

---

[1] Cf. Reiffenstuel, *Jus Canonicum,* Lib. I, tit. 28, nn. 45 sqq.; Barbosa, *Ius Ecclesiasticum,* Lib. III, c. 6, nn. 58 sqq.; Schmalzgrueber, *Jus Ecclesiasticum,* Lib. I. tit. 28, n. 10.

[2] *Jus Canonicum,* Lib. I, tit. 28, n. 23.

[3] Cf. Pirhing, *Jus Canonicum, loc. cit.*

[4] Cf. *supra,* pp. 19 ff.

duties of a pastor in regard to the care of souls.[5] This power as well as the office which he holds comes to him *ipso iure* upon appointment.[6] But neither the power nor the office is conferred upon him for his own consideration or interest. They are given to him that he may be enabled to take care of the spiritual needs of the faithful under the authority of the local ordinary,[7] and in the name of the pastor whose place he is taking.

ARTICLE 1. RIGHTS AND DUTIES.

In order to discharge this important office in the best manner possible, the vicar must definitely know the nature of his rights and the extent of his obligations. The purpose of this chapter, then, will be to determine, in general, just what his rights and duties are.

A. Rights and Prerogatives.

The substitute vicar may be appointed to take the place of the pastor in all things which pertain to the care of souls. This power does not come to him through delegation by the bishop or by the pastor; it is attached to the very office of the vicar. It is ordinary power, even though it is exercised by the vicar not in his own name but in the name of the pastor.[8] Consequently, one of the most important rights of the substitute is his power to delegate others, either to perform a particular act, as, for instance, to assist at a particular marriage, or to give general delegation for all cases,

---

[5] Can. 451, § 2: "Parochis aequiparantur cum omnibus iuribus et obligationibus paroecialibus et parochorum nomine in iure veniunt: . . . 2°. Vicarii paroeciales, si plena potestate paroeciali sint praediti."

[6] Cf. Claeys-Boúúaert, "De Vicario Substituto"—*Jus Pontificium,* VII (1927), 79.

[7] Cf. can. 451, § 1.

[8] Cf. can. 197.

except such regarding which the law expressly provides otherwise.[9]

The principal parochial functions that are reserved to the pastor,[10] and in his absence to the substitute, are recounted in canon 462. They are the following:

1) The Administration of solemn baptism; 2) the carrying of the Blessed Sacrament publicly to the sick; 3) the carrying of Holy Viaticum to the sick, either publicly or privately; 4) the publishing of the banns of matrimony and the announcing of sacred ordinations; 5) the assisting at marriages and the giving of the nuptial blessing; 6) the holding of funeral services according to the norms of canon 1216; 7) the blessing of houses on Holy Saturday or on other days according to custom and according to the norms of the liturgical books; 8) the blessing of the baptismal font on Holy Saturday, the holding of processions outside the church, and the giving of solemn blessings, with pomp and solemnity, outside the church; 9) the right to determine whether a child has the use of reason sufficient for the reception of first Holy Communion.[11]

Rights which are not reserved to the proper pastor, and consequently neither to the vicar who takes the pastor's place, include the following: 1) The right to hear the confessions of the faithful; [12] 2) the right to absolve from cases reserved to the bishop during the paschal season; [13] 3) the right to dispense from the law of fast and abstinence in particular cases; [14] 4) the right to dispense, in specific cases,

---

[9] Can. 199, § 1. Cf. *supra* pp. 11 ff.

[10] Cf. Vermeersch-Creusen, *Epitome,* I, n. 546, ff; Coronata, *Institutiones,* I, 580 ff.

[11] Cf. can. 854, § 5.

[12] Can. 873, § 1. Cf. *infra,* pp. 86 ff.

[13] Can. 899, § 3.

[14] Can. 1245, § 1.

from matrimonial impediments;[15] 5) the right to take the Blessed Sacrament from a non-parochial church in case of a sick call or in order to take Holy Communion to the sick or Holy Viaticum to the dying;[16] and 6) the right to a decent support.

B. Salary

The idea of a cleric receiving his support from his ministry was first expressed by St. Paul when he wrote: "So also the Lord directed that those who preach the gospel should have their living from the gospel."[17] The early jurists developed this idea, so that at the time of Gratian it was already a well-established rule of law that a cleric who faithfully served a church was to receive his living from that church.[18]

This law was further repeated and enlarged upon in the collections of the decretals.[19] During the reign of Alexander III (1159-1181) a dispute arose concerning the salary to be paid the temporary vicar. The Pope, in a response to the Archbishop of Canterbury, made a particular application of the general norms already enacted. He insisted that the temporary vicars were to be given an adequate salary, which was to be taken from the fruits of the benefice, and that these vicars were not to be denied their rights.[20]

---

15 Cans. 1044 and 1045. Cf. *infra*, pp. 67 ff.

16 Can, 483, 2°.

17 I Cor., IX: 14.

18 C. 10, C. 1, q. 2. Cf. *Codex Canonum Ecclesiae Africanae*, XXXIII—Mansi, *Sacrorum Conciliorum Nova et Amplissima Collectio* (53 vols. in 60 Parisiis—Arnhem—Leipzig: 1901-1927), III, 728 (hereafter cited as Mansi).

19 Cf. c. 30, X, *de praebendis et dignitatibus*, III, 5; c. 3, X, *de officio vicarii*, I, 28.

20 C. 4, X, *de officio iudicis ordinarii*, I, 31—Jaffé, *Regesta Pontificum Romanorum ab condita Ecclesia ad annum post Christum natum MCXCVIII* (ed. secundam correctam et auctam aspiciis Gulielmi Watten-

The Council of Trent also demanded that the temporary vicars be given adequate payment [21] from the fruits of the benefice.[22] The exact amount to be paid the temporary vicar was not determined by the Council. But, as in the case of a permanent vicar, the amount depended on the financial condition of the church, the work involved, the place in question, and similar conditions.[23] It was the duty of the bishop in each individual case to determine the exact amount to be paid the vicar.[24]

The question of the salary that is to be paid to a substitute vicar is not treated in the Code. As Claeys-Boúúaert points out,[25] the amount is usually determined by an agreement between the pastor and the vicar, or, in the case specified in canon 1923, § 2, between the bishop and the vicar.[26] If legitimate custom or a diocesan statute determines the precise amount to be paid to the substitute, then that norm is to be followed. Such a regulation supplements

---

bach, curavernunt . . . Löwenfeld, Kaltenbrunner, Ewald, 2 vols. in 1, Lipsiae: 1885-1888), n. 14965 (hereafter cited as JL, JK or JE in designation of the particular editor).

21 Sess. XXIII, *de ref.*, c. 1. "... quandocumque eos curam animarum habentes, causa prius per episcopos cognita et probata, abesse contingerit, vicarium idoneum ab ipso Ordinario approbandum cum debita mercedis assignatione relinquant.". Cf. Laurentius, *Institutiones Iuris Ecclesiastici* (ed. altera, Friburgi: Herder, 1908), Lib. I, tit. 28, n. 45.

22 Conc. Trident., sess VI, *de ref.*, c. 2.

23 Conc. Trident., sess. XXI, *de ref.*, c. 4; S.C.Ep. et Reg., 7 dec. 1691—Ferraris, *Bibliotheca*, ad v. "vicarius parochialis", n. 48.

24 S.C.C., *Mileten.*, 7 iun. 1692—*Fontes*, n. 2931. Cf. Ferraris, *Bibliotheca*, ad v. "vicarius parochialis", n. 48.

25 "De Vicario Substituto"—*Jus Pontificium*, VII (1927), 80.

26 Cf. Beste, *Introductio*, ad can. 474; Ayrinhac, *Constitution of the Church*, pp. 357 ff.

the Church's universal law, and hence is not contrary to it.[27]

C. Duties and Obligations

In order to safeguard the parishioners' right to a proper pastoral care, the Code determines in detail the obligations of the pastor and of those who take the place of the pastor.[28] At this point the nature and the extent of the substitute's obligations will not be treated at length. That will be done in the following chapters. The duties of the pastor and of the substitute will merely be indicated at this point.

The obligations of the pastor and of the substitute who takes the pastor's place are: 1) Residence; [29] 2) sometimes the application of the *Missa pro populo;* [30] 3) the celebration of the divine offices, the administration of the sacraments to the faithful, the duty of knowing and of prudently correcting erring parishioners, of looking after the poor, and of seeing to the proper Catholic education of the youth of the parish; [31] 4) the care of the sick;[32] 5) the keeping of the parish books; [33] and, as for the substitute vicar, in rare instances, 6) the making of the profession of faith.[34]

---

[27] Cf. *Acta et Decreta Concilii Plenarii Americae Latinae in Urbe Celebrati Anno Domini MDCCCXCIX* (Romae: Typis Polyglottis Vaticanis, 1902), n. 270.

[28] Can. 474.

[29] Cf. *supra*, pp. 5 ff.

[30] Can. 466, § 1. Cf. *infra*, pp. 53 ff.

[31] Can. 467, 1. Cf. *infra*, pp. 79 ff.; 92 ff.

[32] Can. 468, 1. Cf. *infra*, pp. 46 ff.

[33] Can. 470, 1. Cf. *infra*, pp. 71, 74, 82, 86.

[34] Cf. Canavan, *Profession of Faith,* The Catholic University of America Canon Law Studies, n. 151 (Washington, D.C.: The Catholic University of America Press, 1942), p. 81. This author agrees that if any limitation at all is placed on the vicar, even a limitation on his salary, it excuses him

D. Stole Fees.

Since the substitute vicar has all the obligations of the pastor in regard to the care of souls, it is necessary to determine who is to receive the stole fees that are offered on the occasion of the administration of the sacraments.[35]

It is not necessary to treat of the reason for the existence of stole fees, of the obligation resting upon the faithful to offer them, of the customs or the laws that determine them, or of the safeguards that the Church has set up to keep them free from any simoniacal aspects. Nor is it necessary to treat of their historical development and evolution. These questions have already been scholarly investigated and may elsewhere be seen in their substantially clarified presentation and solution.[36]

It will be beneficial, however, to restate briefly the existing law regarding stole fees.

The amount of a stole fee may be determined either by means of legitimate custom[37] or through an act of a provincial council whose decrees have been reviewed by the Holy See.[38] A pastor may not exact more than custom or statute allows. If he does so, he is bound to make restitution,[39] and he is liable to the penalties stated in canon 2408.[40]

If a member of the faithful voluntarily offers more than

---

from making the profession of faith. He states also that only in extraordinary circumstances will the profession of faith have to be taken by the substitute vicar.

35 Cf. cans. 463, § 1; 1507. § 1.

36 Cf. Ferry, *Stole Fees,* The Catholic University of America Canon Law Studies, n. 59 (Washington, D.C.: The Catholic University of America, 1930).

37 Can. 463, § 1.

38 Can. 1507, § 1. Cf. can. 736.

39 Can. 463, § 2.

40 Cf. Fanfani, *De Iure Parochorum,* n. 182.

the usual stipend, it may be accepted. If a priest other than the pastor administers a sacrament, the usual stole fee as well as the excess cedes to the pastor, unless it can be established with certainty that the offerer intended the minister, and not the pastor, to receive the surplus amount.

It is the will of the Church that the faithful should pay these legitimate fees whenever possible. It is likewise the will of the Church that gratuitous service should be given to those who are unable to pay the established fees, for the pastor is obliged to furnish his ministrations freely to those beyond whose capacity it is to make a payment.[41] So it may now be asked whether the pastor who leaves his parish in charge of a substitute vicar automatically relinquishes his right to the stole fees. And may the vicar, who takes the pastor's place, consider himself as entitled to receive the stole fees in place of the pastor?

This important problem is not difficult of solution. The answer lies in canon 463, 3, which states: "Licet paroeciale aliquod officium ab alio fuerit expletum, praestationes tamen parocho cedunt, nisi de contraria offerentium voluntate certo constet circa summam quae taxam excedit."

It seems evident, therefore, that the customary offerings as well as the excess that is given out of generosity must be given to the pastor, unless with reference to the surplus amount the contrary is the evident will of the donor. But in no case may the vicar keep both the ordinary stipend as well as the excess, even though that be the explicit intention of the offerer. The pastor is entitled to the usual offering in every case, unless he has explicitly or implicitly relinquished that right to the vicar.[42]

---

[41] Can. 463, § 4.

[42] Claeys-Boúúaert, "De Vicario Substituto"—*Jus Pontificium,* VII (1927), 81: "Adhuc minus substituto per se competit jus ad praestationes seu oblationes quae parocho obveniunt, licet paroeciale officium ab ipso substituto fuerit expletum (c. 463, § 3)." Cf. Ferry, *Stole Fees,* p. 46; Piontek, "A Gentleman's Agreement"—*The Jurist,* III (1943), 298 ff.

But neither may the pastor demand the amount in excess of the usual stipend if the donor has expressed that the actual administrator of the sacrament should receive it. In justice the pastor is entitled to only that amount which has been determined by custom or statute, if in a given case the donor has clearly specified that the surplus amount should go to the one who actually administered the sacrament.[43]

ARTICLE 2. LIMITATION OF THE VICAR'S OFFICE

While it is true that a vicar may possess all the rights and duties spoken of in Article 1, it must be remembered that either the ordinary or the pastor is capable of excepting some power from his jurisdiction or of limiting the extent of his obligations.[44] Any exception, however, must be expressly determined. As Claeys-Boúúaert indicates, an exception is not to be presumed or given a wide interpretation, for that would imply a deviation from the condition of things that was established by the general law.[45]

The right that the ordinary has to limit the power of the substitute was affirmed by the Pontifical Commission for the Interpretation of the Code. The Commission was asked whether the substitute could validly and lawfully assist at marriages after the approbation of the ordinary if no limits were placed upon him. The answer was in the affirmative. The Commission was also asked whether the substitute, when appointed by the pastor in consequence of an unexpected and grave cause for absence, could lawfully and validly assist at marriages before the approbation of the ordinary. Here, too, the answer was in the affirmative,

---

[43] Cf. can. 463, § 3.

[44] Can. 474.

[45] "Debet semper expresse determinari, et in dubio non est praesumenda nec late interpretanda, quia exorbitat a rerum conditione per ius commune ordinata."—Claeys-Boúúaert, "De Vicario Substituto"—*Jus Pontificium,* VII (1927), 81.

with the proviso that the ordinary, to whom the designation of the substitute had been made known, had not ordered otherwise.[46]

While all authors agree that the ordinary and the pastor have the right to limit the substitute's power,[47] it must still be determined whether the limitation affects the validity of the act performed in the face of the conditions as set. If the substitute, knowing that an act has been excepted by the pastor or the bishop, nevertheless performs such an act, e.g., the hearing of confessions, is that act to be regarded, by that very fact, as invalid?

Cappello claims that, since the substitute's power is ordinary, it will always remain ordinary just as the power of the vicar general remains ordinary, even though the bishop has reserved some case to himself and the vicar general, in consequence, needs a special mandate in order to act.[48] He further asserts that neither the pastor nor the ordinary can except anything from the power of the substitute under pain of nullity.[49] The reason he gives is that the vicar's power is ordinary.[50]

It is certainly true that the substitute does possess ordinary power. The problem under discussion, however, is not solved by means of such a statement. At this point it

---

46 P.C.I., 14 iul. 1922, ad V, 1°, 4°—*AAS*, XIV (1922), 527-528.

47 Cf. Coronata, *Institutiones*, I, 593; Vermeersch-Creusen, *Epitome*, I, n. 566; Ayrinhac, *Constitution of the Church*, p. 357; Chelodi, *Ius de Personis*, p. 382, footnote 2; Fanfani, *De Iure Parochorum*, n. 251, B, 4.

48 "De Vicario Substituto"—*Periodica*, XIX (1930), 3*. Cf. Roelker, "The Vicar General and the Special Mandate", *The Jurist*, II (1942), 346-362, but especially pp. 354 ff.

49 Cappello, *Summa Iuris Canonici in Usum Scholarum Concinnata* (3 vols., Vol II, Romae: Apud Aedes Universitatis Gregorianae, 1930), II, 556 (hereafter cited as *Summa*).

50 "Parochus *sub poena nullitatis* nihil excipere valet, nec *per se* Ordinarius loci. Potestas vicarii substituti est ordinaria."—Cappello, *Summa*, *loc. cit.*

is necessary to determine, not the quality of power possessed by the substitute vicar, but the amount of ordinary power that he has. And the amount of power that the vicar will have in a particular case is what is precisely determined by the *nisi* clause of canon 474. In other words, if the bishop or the pastor places a restriction on the vicar, for instance, by denying to him the right to hear confessions, then the vicar does not possess ordinary power by reason of his office of substitute vicar to hear confessions for the simple reason that this power has been withheld from him.

If a power is withheld from the vicar it is illogical to contend that such a power still remains a part of the totality from which it is cut off. Cappello, while admitting that the pastor or the ordinary may except something from the jurisdiction of the vicar, seems to make that claim when he refuses to the pastor or the ordinary the right to make a restriction which would affect the validity of the vicar's actions. It appears evident, however, that a restriction placed on the vicar equivalently denotes that a particular right or power is not a part of the totality of the ordinary power from which it has remained dissociated. Thus an act placed by the vicar contrary to the express restrictions of the pastor or the ordinary must be considered as invalid as well as unlawful.

ARTICLE 3. THE TEMPORAL ADMINISTRATION OF THE PARISH BY THE VICAR SUBSTITUTE.

Canon 474 explicitly states that the vicar substitute has full charge of the parish in those things which pertain to the care of souls. The canon gives the vicar absolutely no authority over matters which pertain to the temporal administration of the parish. The authors naturally do not treat of the vicar's competence to administer the goods of the parish, inasmuch as such an administration is not contemplated by the lawgiver. Consequently the vicar, just like the administrator of a vacant parish, is not authorized to perform any act that would prove prejudicial to the interests of the pastor or of the parish.

If the pastor is absent from the parish for a long time, however, the vicar may reasonably presume that he has authority to pay the ordinary expenses of the parish. Such expenses would include the ordinary expenses incurred in running the rectory, the salaries of the hired help, and the like. The vicar should keep a strict account of all such expenses, so that a complete report can be given to the pastor upon his return.

During the pastor's absence it may happen that the vicar is able to make, in his opinion, an extraordinary saving for the parish. The vicar may know that the pastor is contemplating the redecoration of the church, and the vicar may feel able to secure the services of an artist-friend for a nominal fee.

In this, and in all similar cases, the vicar must bear in mind that the church is not under his control, but under the control of the pastor. It is very likely that the pastor has definite ideas about the type of decorating that he wants in the church. Besides this fact, the cost of decorating the church necessarily places a burden upon the congregation, which would have to pay the cost of the decorating, and also upon the pastor, who would have to raise the money to pay the artist. Consequently the vicar who is at the church to care for the spiritual welfare of the parishioners, and not for any other purpose, would be acting very imprudently to arrange to have the church decorated even under the plea of saving money for the congregation.

If it should happen, however, that the sexton or the organist or some other person employed at the church should have died or have sought other employment during the pastor's absence, it seems that the vicar is permitted to hire another to take the place of the one who died or who left the employment of the church. In such a case the vicar should not enter into a long-term contract with the new employee. The vicar should rather stipulate that the work is on a week to week basis until the pastor returns. Upon his return the pastor can negotiate a long-term contract if he so desires.

During his tenure of office the vicar is not permitted to refurnish the church or the rectory, or to attempt to improve the property of the church, unless he has been given explicit permission, preferably in writing, by the pastor. If the church is assessed for public improvements, however, such as occurs when the city installs a new street or sidewalk in the vicinity of the church, the vicar is certainly allowed to pay for such improvements. The church property is not exempt from the making of such payments, for the pastor equally as the vicar could not have escaped the responsibility for the payment of the assessment.

In all matters which pertain to administration the vicar should have as his guiding principle, *nihil innovetur.* Outside of the ordinary expenses of the church and of the rectory, the vicar should incur no debts or obligations. Matters of greater moment, if they must be settled before the pastor's return, should be referred to the bishop. The bishop, knowing the circumstances of the case and the financial condition of the parish, will be able to decide how the best interests of the church can be protected in that particular instance.

CHAPTER IV

The Missa Pro Populo [1]

ARTICLE 1. THE OBLIGATION IN ITSELF.

The obligation of the *missa pro populo* binds all those who have the actual care of souls to apply the fruits of the Sacrifice of the Mass for the faithful entrusted to their care.[2] This obligation which obliges pastors in justice [3] is founded in divine law.[4]

A. Early History

Although no early general legislation explicitly bound those who had the care of souls to offer the holy sacrifice for their flock, still traces of the acknowledged existence of this obligation can be found in Scripture. St. Paul indicated this obligation in the Epistle to the Hebrews: "For every high priest taken from among men is appointed for men in the things pertaining to God, that he may offer gifts and sacrifice for sins . . . and by reason thereof is obliged to offer for sins, as on behalf of the people, so also for himself." [5] The authors consider this text as at least

[1] For a complete historical treatment of the *missa pro populo* cf. Donnellan, *The Obligation of the* Missa pro Populo, The Catholic University of American Canon Law Studies, n. 155 (Washington, D.C.: The Catholic University of America Press, 1942), pp. 1-44 (hereafter cited as *The* Missa pro Populo).

[2] Cf. Donnellan, *The* Missa pro Populo, p. 1.

[3] Cf. Coronata, *Institutiones,* I, 585; Vermeersch-Creusen, *Epitome,* I, n. 553.

[4] Cf. Benedictus XIV, ep. encycl. *Cum semper oblatas,* 19 aug. 1774—*Fontes,* n. 345; Conc. Trident., sess. XXIII, *de ref.,* c. 1.

[5] Heb., V; 1 ff.

implicitly commanding that sacrifice be offered for the faithful.[6]

The first law having general and universal application, however, was not enacted until the Council of Trent. The Fathers of the Council, after a lengthy and spirited discussion about the exact nature of the obligation,[7] finally decreed: Cum precepto divino mandatum sit omnibus quibus animarum cura commissa est, oves suas agnoscere, pro his sacrificium offerre . . . Synodus eos admonet et horatur, ut divinorum praeceptorum memores, facti forma gregis, in veritate pascant et regant.[8]

This decree, while indicating that those who had the care of souls were obliged to offer the Sacrifice of the Mass for their people, did not precisely specify whether the obligation was one of celebrating Mass for the convenience of the people or whether the Mass was to be applied by way of intention for the spiritual benefit of the people. This dispute among the authors was settled by a decision of the Sacred Congregation of the Council in 1628. The Council explicitly stated that the Mass was to be celebrated and the fruits of the Mass were to be applied in behalf of the faithful.[9] The same Congregation at that time also declared that the pastor could not fulfill both the obligations as arising from an accepted stipend and as deriving from the *missa pro populo* through the celebration of a single Mass.[10]

---

[6] Cf. Donnellan, *The* MISSA PRO POPULO, p. 4.

[7] Cf. Donnellan, *op. cit.*, pp. 13 ff.

[8] Sess. XXIII, *de ref.*, c. 1.

[9] S.C.C., *Civitatis Castellanae,* 26 aug. 1628: "Parochi enim diebus Festis et Dominicis tenentur celebrare et Sacrificium applicare pro ovibus suis . . ." Pallottini, *Collectio omnium conclusionum et resolutionum S. Cong. Concilii* (18 vols., Romae, 1868-1893), XIV, "Parochus", VI, n. 68 (hereafter cited as Pallottini).

[10] S.C.C., *Civitatis Castellanae,* 26 aug. 1628, *loc. cit.*

Despite these explicit decisions many pastors did not fully understand the nature and the extent of their obligation.[11] To remedy this situation and to clarify the exact obligation imposed on those who had the care of souls, Benedict XIV (1740-1758) issued an encyclical letter, which he directed to all the bishops of Italy.[12] This encyclical, which was issued on August 19, 1744, specified that everyone who had the actual care of souls was obliged to celebrate the *missa pro populo* on Sundays and days of precept.[13]

Except for further clarification of the times when the pastor was obligated to celebrate the *missa pro populo,* very little development occurred until the promulgation of the present Code of Canon Law.[14]

B. The Present Law.

According to most of the authors, the obligation of celebrating the *missa pro populo* as imposed upon the pastor has four separate and distinct characteristics.[15] It is first of all a *real obligation,* for even if the pastor, in view of a just cause, cannot say the Mass himself, the obligation remains until it is satisfied on another day or by another priest.[16] Secondly, it is a *personal obligation* on the part of the pastor, for he must say the Mass himself unless he is

---

[11] Cf. Donnellan, *The* MISSA PRO POPULO, pp. 26 ff.

[12] The S.C.C. soon extended the decrees of the encyclical *Cum semper oblatas* to places outside of Italy. Cf. S.C.C., *in Caliguritana,* 12 dec. 1767—*Thesaurus Resolutionum Sacrae Congregationis Concilii* (167 vols, Romae, 1718-1908), XXXVI, 214 ff. (hereafter cited *Thesaurus*).

[13] § IV—*Fontes,* n. 345.

[14] Cf. Donnellan, *The* MISSA PRO POPULO, pp. 29 ff.

[15] Cf. Noldin, *Summa Theologiae Moralis iuxta Codicem Iuris Canonici Scholarum Usui Accommodavit A. Schmitt* (3 vols., Vol. III, *De Sacramentis,* 25 ed., Oeniponte: Rauch, 1938), III, n. 184 ff. (hereafter cited as *De Sacramentis*); Donnellan, *The* MISSA PRO POPULO, pp. 54 ff.

[16] Cf. can. 446, § 1.

legitimately impeded or legitimately absent.[17] Thirdly, it is a *local obligation,* inasmuch as it must be celebrated in the parish church unless circumstances demand or persuade otherwise.[18] Lastly, the obligation is *affixed to a certain day,* so that the application of the Mass must take place on that day unless the ordinary, for a just cause, permits the obligation to be transferred to another day.[19]

The pastor has a grave obligation to celebrate or to have celebrated the *missa pro populo,* and it is commonly accepted that the deliberate omission of even one such Mass is a grave sin.[20] The secondary obligations, however, such as the application of the Mass on the specified day, or its celebration by the pastor, or in the parish church, do not oblige under grave sin unless they are violated frequently, or, as Noldin states, "*fere ex consuetudine violentur.*"[21]

ARTICLE 2. THE OBLIGATION OF THE SUBSTITUTE VICAR

Canon 466, § 1, states that the pastor must celebrate the *missa pro populo.* Authors agree that the obligation is constituted a personal one for the pastor.[22] Canon 474, however, prescribes that a substitute vicar who is legitimately appointed takes the place of the pastor in all things that pertain to the care of souls unless the ordinary or the pastor excepts some right or duty from his care.

---

17 Cf. can. 466, § 5.

18 Cf. can. 466, § 4.

19 Cf. can. 466, § 3.

20 Cf. Noldin, *De Sacramentis,* n. 183, d.

21 *De Sacramentis, loc cit.* Cf. Davis, *Moral and Pastoral Theology* (4 vols., Vol. III, *Sacraments,* 3 ed., London: Sheed and Ward, 1938), III, 108.

22 Cf. Cappello, *Summa,* II, n. 529; Fanfani, *De Iure Parochorum,* n. 362.

If the pastor, therefore, explicitly states that he will say the *missa pro populo* wherever he will be, the substitute certainly does not have the obligation. When the vicar is told that he has full charge of the parish, with all rights and duties, inasmuch as the absent pastor wants to be free of all parochial cares, the substitute is certainly bound to celebrate the *missa pro populo.*

The difficulty, then, arises only when nothing is said to the vicar about this obligation. Advertence, possibly, is not given to the obligation in the rush of last minute preparations on the part of the pastor, or the latter may perhaps assume that the vicar will, or will not say the Mass, as the case may be. In such a case the vicar will have to determine whether or not he should consider himself obligated to celebrate the *missa pro populo,* even though he has received no definite instructions from the pastor.

In order to clarify the issue, a fictitious case may be considered. Fr. X is appointed as the approved substitute to take the place of a pastor who will be absent from his parish for three months. The pastor, who leaves the parish before Fr. X's arrival, does not leave any specific instructions. He believes that since he has a country parish no special reservations of power and no specific commands are called for.

Fr. X upon his arrival finds the ordinary's letter which states that he has all the rights and duties of a substitute during the pastor's absence. After reading the letter Fr. X wonders whether he is obliged to say the *missa pro populo,* since he is taking the place of the pastor in all things.

Two solutions are offered. One opinion claims that the substitute is under the obligation of saying the Mass; the other opinion contends that he is free of it.

A. Argument Against the Claim of the Substitute's Obligation.

Donnellan states that the consensus among authors is that a grave fault is committed by one who has charge of the care of souls if he frequently has the *missa pro populo* celebrated by a substitute.[23] It is evident, however, from the authors he quotes,[24] that he is not using the term " substitute " in the strict canonical sense, but in the sense of any priest who fulfills the primary obligation of the pastor of applying the *missa pro populo.*

Donnellan does state in another place that the obligation of saying the *missa pro populo* remains with the pastor unless he has expressly delegated it to the substitute. He argues: " The only reason why he [the substitute vicar] is not bound to the application of the Mass for the people is the personal nature of the obligation, which remains the pastor's unless, in legitimate absence, the latter wishes to take advantage of the privilege granted him by can. 466, § 5, of satisfying his obligation through the priest who takes his place in the parish." [25]

Most of the authors who uphold the pastor's continued personal obligation of saying the *missa pro populo* even after a substitute has been appointed make use of this same argument.[26]

---

[23] *The* MISSA PRO POPULO, p. 57.

[24] Noldin, *De Sacramentis*, n. 183; Davis, *Moral and Pastoral Theology*, III, 108; Lehmkuhl, *Theologia Moralis*, (2 vols., 11 ed., Friburgi Brisgoviae, 1910), II, n. 196 and others.

[25] *The* MISSA PRO POPULO, p. 62.

[26] Fanfani, *De Iure Parochorum*, n. 362: " Excluduntur . . . etiam *vicarii substituti*, cum obligatio applicandi Missam pro populo in ipso parocho adiuto vel substituto remaneat." Vermeersch-Creusen, *Epitome*, I, n. 553: " Hac obligatione tenentur parochi; Vicarius curatus; Vicarius oeconomus; Vicarius parocho absenti substitutus, ex condicto tantum cum parocho."

B. Argument Against the Claim of the Pastor's Obligation.

There are very few authors who argue that the pastor is not obliged to celebrate the *missa pro populo* even after the appointment of a substitute vicar. Claeys-Boúúaert, however, in his article on the substitute vicar, expressly states that the vicar is bound by the obligation of saying the Mass, and not the pastor.[27]

This author gives his solution in the form of a question and answer. In the case wherein nothing is said to the substitute vicar about celebrating the *missa pro populo,* he asks whether the presumption is that the substitute must say the mass or may rightfully forego doing so. After citing two authors who deny that the substitute has the obligation, Claeys-Boúúaert states it to be his opinion that in such circumstances the substitute is bound to celebrate the *missa pro populo.* Two reasons are given in support of his opinion: 1) The general wording of canon 474; and 2) the fact that the substitute has ample competence given him by the law, which circumstance seems to indicate that the pastor renounces the option he has of saying the Mass at the place where he is staying,[28] unless he expressly reserves the fulfillment of this option to himself.[29]

C. Evaluation of the Two Opinions.

Canon 18 states that ecclesiastical laws are to be understood according to the proper signification of the words used, considered in their text and context. If this norm be

---

27 " De Vicario Substituto "—*Jus Pontificium,* VII (1927), 79 ff.

28 Cf. can. 466, § 5.

29 " Censemus potius affirmandum, propter verba generalia c. 474, et quia, data ampla substituti competentia a jure stabilita, parochus renunciare videtur facultati celebrandi in loco ubi degit, *nisi hanc expresse sibi reservaverit.*"—Claeys-Boúúaert, " De Vicario Substituto "—*Jus Pontificium,* VII (1927). 79 ff.

applied to canon 474, wherein it is stated that the substitute takes the place of the pastor in all things that pertain to the care of souls, it seems that by the law the presumption is simply that the substitute whose power is not limited by the pastor or by the ordinary must take the place of the pastor in all things. The *missa pro populo* is certainly part of the *cura animarum,*[30] and consequently must be presumptively included in the sphere of the substitute's obligations, unless conclusive arguments can be brought forth to overthrow the presumption established by the law.

Those who contend that the pastor is obliged to apply the *missa pro populo* unless he expressly charges his vicar to do so, rightly consider the *missa pro populo* as a personal obligation incumbent on the pastor. This deduction is based on the wording of canon 339, which states in part that the bishop, or in the present case the pastor, is obliged to apply the *missa pro populo per se ipse.*[31]

The authors who uphold the claim of the substitute's obligation unless the pastor expressly reserved the execution of this obligation to himself do not deny that the pastor has a personal obligation of celebrating the *missa pro populo.* They do contend, however, that it is not so personal that presumptively the obligation follows him wherever he goes. This does not imply the attaching of an arbitrary meaning to the word "personal"; it is but an interpretation that is sanctioned by the law itself. Canon 466, § 5, allows the pastor who is legitimately absent to celebrate the Mass where he is, but it also allows him to have it celebrated by another priest who takes his place.

At the same time, however, canon 466, § 4, indicates that it is the pastor who is obliged to offer the *missa pro populo*

---

[30] Cf. Vermeersch-Creusen, *Epitome,* I, n. 550.

[31] Can 466, § 1, states that the pastor is obliged to apply the *missa pro populo* according to the norms of can. 339.

in the parish church "*nisi rerum adiuncta Missam alibi celebrandam exigant aut suadeant.*" Consequently, even if the pastor is away from the parish church he is obliged to offer the *missa pro populo.*[32]

It may be further argued against the claim of the substitute's obligation that canon 466, § 5, states that the pastor who is legitimately absent is allowed (*potest*) to celebrate personally the *missa pro populo* wherever he is, or may have it celebrated by the priest who is taking his place in the parish. It seems that if the pastor is allowed to choose whether he will say the Mass personally or through another, that the substitute does not automatically inherit the obligation by the very fact that he takes over the pastor's office.[33]

It may be argued in rebuttal that it is not denied that the pastor still has the right to make this choice, but that it is simply contended that this choice must be made known to the substitute. If the vicar is not so notified he can legitimately presume that the pastor wishes him to fulfill the obligation of the *missa pro populo.*

Such a presumption, however, seems entirely unwarranted. The vicar is not certain that the pastor wants him to apply the *missa pro populo,* and consequently the existence of the obligation on the substitute is also uncertain. In such a case the vicar is obliged to apply the principle "*lex incerta non obligat.*"

If the vicar is obliged to say the *missa pro populo* then the pastor is forced to choose to have the mass offerred by the substitute. In such a case, the option that is granted to the pastor in canon 466, § 5, would be ineffective and inoperative. To insist that the pastor's silence in this matter

---

32 Cf. Bastnagel, "The Parochial Vicar Substitute and the *Missa Pro Populo*", *The Jurist,* VII (1947), 65 ff.

33 Cf. Beste, *Introductio,* ad can. 474.

implies that he wants to fulfill this obligation, not personally, but through a substitute, does not seem warranted from the arguments advanced.

It must be kept in mind that from the earliest centuries of the Church the Popes have insisted that the *missa pro populo* should be said by the one having the care of souls and on the day when the obligation occurs. When the pastor is present at the parish there is no difficulty in this matter; if he is unable to say the Mass himself he can have it said by another.

When the pastor is absent from his parish, however, it could easily happen that he might be impeded from celebrating the *missa pro populo*. When this possibility occurs the Code of Canon Law provides that the pastor who has the personal obligation of applying the *missa pro populo* must arrange to have the mass celebrated. This seems to be the more feasible manner of solving the difficulty, for it safeguards the pastor's right to say the mass at a place other than the parish church, and also his right to offer the mass personally or through another.

CHAPTER V

Assistance at Marriage

The substitute vicar, once legitimately appointed, takes the place of the pastor in all things that pertain to the care of souls,[1] which certainly includes the right to administer the sacraments to the faithful.[2] The authors once disputed whether this general power of the vicar also included the right to assist at marriages. Now there is no longer room for dispute since the difficulty has been authoritatively solved by a decision of the Pontifical Commission for the Interpretation of the Code.

The Commission was asked four questions. The questions were worded in such a way as to cover all possible cases that might arise. The first question asked whether the substitute vicar mentioned in canon 465, § 4, could lawfully and validly assist at marriages, after the approbation of the ordinary had been obtained, as long as no limitation had been placed upon his powers. The Commission's answer was in the affirmative. The second question as proposed dealt with the case of a substitute who was appointed by the pastor in a case of non-urgent absence, but without the approval of the ordinary. The Commission was asked whether such a vicar could lawfully and validly assist at marriages. To this question the Commission gave a negative answer. The third question asked whether the vicar of a religious pastor could validly assist at marriages after the approval of the ordinary had been obtained, but

1 Can. 474.

2 Cf. Claeys-Boúúaert, "De Vicario Substituto"—*Jus Pontificium*, VII (1927), 81.

before the religious superior had given his approval. This question received an affirmative answer. Finally the Commission was interrogated whether the vicar who was appointed by the pastor in consequence of an unforeseen and urgent cause could validly and lawfully assist at marriages before the ordinary had given his approval. The Commission replied in the affirmative contingently on the fact that the ordinary has not provided otherwise in the case.[3]

It can be concluded, therefore, that the only limits imposed on a validly appointed substitute are those which are imposed by the general law on the pastor, if the case is one in which nothing has been expressly excepted from the sphere of his powers.[4]

ARTICLE 1. THE VICAR'S RIGHTS AND DUTIES REGARDING MARRIAGES.

A. Acts Preceding and Following the Marriage Ceremony.

Since the substitute takes the place of the pastor, it is necessary for him to observe the same laws which the pastor must observe regarding assistance at marriages. So, while of anyone within the limits of the parish, yet in order to act the vicar, like the pastor, can assist validly at the marriage lawfully he must first determine the free status of the parties and comply with the other general laws of the Code as well as the particular laws enacted by the bishop for his diocese.

The general procedure to be followed by the vicar, therefore, is as follows:

1) The vicar must be morally certain that the parties are free to contract marriage.[5] Knowledge of the free state of

---

[3] P.C.I., 14 iul. 1922—*AAS,* XIV (1922), 527-528.

[4] Cf. can. 1095, § 1.

[5] Can. 1097, § 1, 1°.

the parties may be gained from an interrogation of the parties themselves, from the evidence of documents, from the publication of the banns in the parish church or, if necessary, from the testimony of the parties or witnesses taken under oath.[6]

2) If the substitute is called upon to assist at a mixed marriage[7] he must always have the parties sign the usual promises. These promises point to the Catholic party's continued freedom to practice his religion, and to the event that all children born of the marriage will be baptized and educated in the Catholic faith.[8]

3) If neither of the parties has a domicile, a quasi-domicile, or a month's residence in the parish, the vicar must obtain permission to assist at the marriage from the proper pastor.[9] Ordinarily this permission is given by the pastor of the bride.[10]

4) If both parties of the marriage are Catholics, the vicar must see that notice of the forthcoming marriage is sent to all proper pastors, so that they may also publish the banns of marriage. This must be done in all cases unless a dispensation from the banns is obtained from the bishop.[11]

If one party is a non-Catholic, the banns are not to be published unless the ordinary, in a particular case, permits them to be announced upon a previous act of dispensation

---

[6] Cf. Cappello, *Tractatus Canonico-Moralis de Sacramentis* (3 vols., Vol. III, *De Matrimonio,* 3. ed., Taurini: Marietti, 1933), III, n. 147 (hereafter cited *De Matrimonio*); Ramstein, *The Pastor and Marriage Cases* (2 ed., New York: Benziger Bros., 1938), n. 46.

[7] Cf. cans. 1060; 1070.

[8] Cf. cans. 1061, § 1; 1071.

[9] Cf. can. 1097, § 1, 3°.

[10] Cf. Ramstein, *The Pastor and Marriage Cases,* n. 46.

[11] Can. 1022. Cf. *infra,* pp. 76 ff.

of mixed religion or of disparity of cult granted by the Holy See.[12]

5) When the vicar discovers an impediment which would prevent or impede the valid celebration of the marriage, he must apply to the ordinary for a dispensation.[13]

6) Before he assists at the marriage the vicar must secure the baptismal certificates of the parties, even if one was baptized as a non-Catholic. If it is impossible to secure such a certificate, he must secure the testimony of at least one reliable witness. Under the same circumstances the sworn testimony of the party himself, however, may be accepted if he was baptized in adult age.[14]

7) If it is necessary to consult the ordinary of the place because of the circumstances of the case,[15] this should be done in due time before the marriage.

8) When the vicar discovers through questioning the parties of a Catholic marriage that they are ignorant of the elements of their religion, he is obliged to instruct them before proceeding with the marriage.[16] If they refuse to take the instructions, however, the vicar cannot, for that reason alone, refuse to assist at the marriage.[17]

When the proposed marriage is to be contracted between a Catholic and a non-Catholic, the diocesan statutes may prescribe that a definite number of instructions must be given before a dispensation will be granted. Such laws will have to be observed for at least the lawfulness of the act of assistance at the marriage.

---

12 Can. 1026.

13 Cf. cann. 1058-1080.

14 Cf. can. 779.

15 Cf. cann. 1023, § 2; 1026; 1031, § 1, 3°; 1032; 1034; 1063, § 2; 1065, § 2; 1066; 1102, § 2; 1104-1107; 1108, § 3; 1109, § 2.

16 Can. 1020, § 2.

17 P.C.I., 2 iun. 1918; *AAS*, X (1918), 345.

9) After the wedding the vicar must record the marriage in the marriage register,[18] and he must notify the pastors of the parishes where the parties were baptized, so that the proper notification of the marriage may be made in the margin of the baptismal record.[19]

B. The Substitute Vicar and Canons 1044-1045.

Besides the faculty of assisting at marriages, the vicar is also endowed with the power of dispensing from certain matrimonial impediments in specified cases. These cases are mentioned in canons 1044 and 1045.[20]

1. Danger of Death—Canon 1044.

In a case wherein danger of death is involved for one or both of the parties and wherein timely recourse to the local ordinary cannot be made, the pastor or the substitute vicar who takes the place of the pastor is given the extraordinary power of dispensing from matrimonial impediments.[21] The conditions under which this power may be exercised are explicitly stated in the canons.

First of all the case must involve the danger of death for one of the parties. Cappello asserts that this danger is present when the circumstances are such that it is problematical whether the person will live or die, either alternative being probable in the case.[22] Therefore it is not

---

18 Can. 1103, § 1.

19 Can. 1103, § 2.

20 For a complete treatment of these canons cf. O'Keeffe, *Matrimonial Dispensations, Powers of Bishops, Priests and Confessors,* The Catholic University of America Canon Law Studies, n. 45 (Washington, D.C.: The Catholic University of America, 1927), pp. 102-185 (hereafter cited *Matrimonial Dispensations*). Cf. Cappello, *De Matrimonio,* nn. 236 ff.; Ramstein, *The Pastor and Marriage Cases,* nn. 63 ff.

21 Cf. Cappello, *De Matrimonio,* n. 236.

22 Cappello, *De Matrimonio,* n. 231.

necessary for the vicar to wait until the person is *in articulo mortis* before he may exercise his power of dispensing.[23] All that is required is that the vicar make a moral estimate or appraisal of the danger involved. This danger may be occasioned either by intrinsic causes, such as sickness or old age, or it may arise from extrinsic causes, such as may occur when a person must undergo a dangerous operation or when a soldier is sent to the battlefield.[24]

The second condition is that there be some necessity for adjusting matters of conscience and, if the case demands it, for effecting the legitimation of the offspring.[25]

While the fulfillment of this condition is requisite for the validity of the dispensation,[26] it is not postulated that both reasons be present at the same time. It is the common opinion that the presence of either of the two reasons is sufficient for the exercise of this power.[27] It is likewise a safe opinion that the power of dispensing may be used when not the dying person but the healthy party of the marriage is disturbed in conscience.[28] Such a case is possible when there is question of a mixed marriage in which the non-Catholic party is dying and the Catholic party desires to have the marriage convalidated.

The third condition is that the vicar be unable to have recourse to the local ordinary.[29] The canon does not imply that physically it must be absolutely impossible to approach the ordinary. The emphasis must rather be placed on the

---

[23] Cf. O'Keeffe, *Matrimonial Dispensations*, p. 56.

[24] Cf. Cappello, *De Matrimonio*, n. 231.

[25] Can. 1043.

[26] Cf. O'Keeffe, *Matrimonial Dispensations*, p. 59.

[27] Cf. Cappello, *De Matrimonio*, n. 231; O'Keeffe, *Matrimonial Dispensations*, p. 59.

[28] Cf. O'Keeffe, *Matrimonial Dispensations*, p. 62.

[29] Can. 1044.

danger that the person will die or lapse into unconsciousness while the recourse is being made.[30] The moral impossibility of approaching the ordinary in time is all that is required.[31]

When these three conditions are present the vicar can dispense from the form, that is, the formalities that are ordinarily prescribed by the Church for the celebration of marriage. Thus the vicar could dispense from the necessity of having a priest present for the marriage. He could dispense from the presence of witnesses. He could dispense from the requisite presence of both priest and witnesses if the case warranted it.[32]

The vicar is likewise empowered to dispense from practically all matrimonial impediments which have been enacted purely as ecclesiastical law.[33] This includes diriment and prohibitive impediments, whether public or occult, multiple or simple. Just two exceptions are made. They are the impediments arising from the sacred order of priesthood and from affinity in the direct line when the marriage which gave rise to the relationship has been consummated. In these two cases the vicar is not empowered to permit the celebration of marriage even in danger of death on the side of either or both of the parties.

Whenever the vicar uses this faculty, however, he must take precautions to see that all scandal be kept removed in

---

30 Cf. Ramstein, *The Pastor and Marriage Cases,* n. 63; O'Keeffe, *op. cit.,* p. 104.

31 Cf. O'Keeffe, *op. cit.,* p. 105.

32 Cf. O'Keeffe, *Matrimonial Dispensations,* pp. 72 ff.; Motry, *Diocesan Faculties According to the Code of Canon Law.* The Catholic University of America Canon Law Studies, n. 16 (Washington, D.C.: The Catholic University of America, 1923), pp. 131 ff.

33 The vicar, of course, cannot dispense from impediments arising from the divine law, such as *ligamen* or the existence of a prior validly contracted marriage, certain and absolute impotency, consanguinity in the direct line, and the like.

the case. Possible scandal that could arise because of any mistaken belief that the parties are still living in concubinage can be forestalled by making the validation of the marriage known to those, who without such knowledge, would continue to be scandalized. If scandal would arise through the very fact that a particular marriage has been contracted, for example, the marriage of an ordained deacon, then it is indicated that upon recovery from the danger of death the parties be instructed to move to some other locality or to avail themselves of other measures equally effective for the allaying of all possible scandal.[34]

If the vicar uses his faculties to validate a mixed marriage by dispensing from the impediment of mixed religion or of disparity of cult, it is prescribed that he must exact the usual promises or guarantees. It seems evident, however, that if explicit promises cannot be obtained, implicit guarantees will suffice. Thus, if the Catholic party has always been free to exercise his religion and the children already born have been given baptism and are receiving a Catholic education, it seems legitimate to conclude that the guarantees exist at least implicitly.[35] If it should happen however, that the non-Catholic party is absolutely opposed to the Catholic baptism and education of the children, and the priest cannot be morally certain that the requirements of divine law will be satisfied, then he is unable to make valid use of the faculties given him in canon 1044.[36]

When all the conditions prescribed by law as explained above are fulfilled, the vicar can dispense in both the in-

---

[34] Cf. O'Keeffe, *Matrimonial Dispensations*, p. 81.

[35] Cf. Boyle, *The Juridic Effect of Moral Certitude on Pre-nuptial Guarantees*, The Catholic University of America Canon Law Studies, n. 150 (Washington, D.C.: The Catholic University of America Press, 1942), pp. 53-58, 162-166.

[36] Cf. Boyle, *The Juridic Effect of Moral Certitude on Pre-nuptial Guarantees*, p. 165.

ternal and the external forum. Moreover, he may use his faculties in order to convalidate marriages already invalidly contracted or in order to prepare the way for the simple contracting of valid marriages.

Since the law makes no distinction or exception, it must be held that the power of the vicar can be used in favor of all parishioners, wherever they may be. It can also be used in favor of dispensing all those who are actually living within the parish at the time.[37]

After the vicar has actually dispensed from the form or from one or more impediments, the fact must be made known to the local ordinary. It is likewise prescribed that a notation of the dispensation be made in the matrimonial register.[38] If, in view of a secret impediment, the dispensation was granted in the internal non-sacramental forum alone, then no public report is to be made to the diocesan chancery, but the fact is to be recorded in the proper book in the secret archives of the diocese.[39] This record will later suffice to furnish proof in the external forum that the impediment had been removed. The availability of such proof serves an imperative precaution in the possible event that the validity of the marriage were ever attacked at a later time by either of the parties.

2. Urgent Cases—Canon 1045.

When all preparations have been made for a marriage and an impediment is discovered at a time when the ceremony cannot be postponed until a dispensation can be obtained from the proper public authority because of a lack of time or for fear of violating a secret, the pastor or vicar, in an occult case, may dispense from all impediments of the

[37] Cf. O'Keeffe, *Matrimonial Dispensations*, p. 107.

[38] Can. 1046.

[39] Cf. can. 1047.

ecclesiastical law except those which arise from the sacred order of priesthood or from affinity in the direct line when the marriage which gave rise to the relationship has been consummated.[40]

It is easily seen that there are three conditions which must be present before this faculty may be used. First, the case must be an urgent one in the sense that all preparations have been made for the wedding, so that the marriage cannot be postponed without probable danger of grave harm. The grave harm, however, does not include the remedying of already existing evils, such as the rectifying of a marriage which is invalid since it was contracted in the face of an existing diriment impediment. The grave harm refers only to evils which possibly will emerge if the marriage is not celebrated at this particular time.[41]

The impending evil result may be either of a spiritual or of a temporal nature. It is not necessary that the vicar have moral certitude that grave harm would result; a prudent fear that such an evil will emerge is a sufficient reason for warranting the use of his faculty in order to grant the needed dispensation.[42]

Is a case, however, to be considered as urgent if the parties indeed knew of the impediment before, but only at the last moment made it known to the pastor? The Pontifical Commission for the Interpretation of the Code, when asked this question, responded that as long as all things had been prepared for the wedding the pastor (and consequently the vicar) could dispense.[43] The condition is verified when the wedding is so imminent that it must be celebrated within a

---

[40] Can. 1045, § 2.

[41] Cf. Bouscaren, *Canon Law Digest,* II, ad can. 1045.

[42] Cf. O'Keeffe, *Matrimonial Dispensations,* p. 133.

[43] P.C.I., 1 mart. 1921—*AAS,* XIII (1921), 177.

shorter time than that which in the case is required to obtain the needed dispensation from the local ordinary.[44]

According to a probable opinion, too, the preparations referred to in this canon include not only the canonical preparations, such as the completed publication of the banns, or the detailed fulfillment of the other formalities required by law,[45] but also the non-canonical preparations, such as the selection of a certain day by the parties, the sending of wedding invitations, and the like.[46]

Secondly, the case must be occult in point of fact. Formerly the authors disputed whether the impediment had to be occult also in its nature, or whether it had to be occult simply in fact. This dispute has been authoritatively settled by the Pontifical Interpretation Commission. This Commission determined that, even though the impediment be public in its nature, the pastor may dispense as long as the impediment has remained occult in fact.[47]

Thirdly, the vicar must be unable to secure the proper dispensation from the ordinary, either because no sufficient time remains for him to do so, or because there would be danger of the violating of a secret.

For the securing of the dispensation from the local ordinary the vicar is not under any legal constraint to employ extraordinary means, such as the telegraph or the telephone. The Pontifical Commission has determined that only ordinary means need to be used in the effort of procuring the needed dispensation.[48]

If there be danger of the violation of secrecy, whether in its character it be sacramental, professional or natural, the

---

[44] Cf. Bouscaren, *Canon Law Digest,* II, ad can. 1045.

[45] Cf. cans. 1020 to 1033.

[46] Cf. O'Keeffe, *loc. cit.*

[47] P.C.I., 28 dec. 1927—*AAS,* XX (1928), 61.

[48] P.C.I., 12 nov. 1922—*AAS,* XIV (1922), 662.

priest is altogether excused from having recourse for obtaining the dispensation from the local ordinary.[49]

When the substitute vicar dispenses from an impediment in the external forum, the fact that a dispensation was granted must be noted in the marriage register.[50] In the case of a secret which both of its nature and also in fact is occult, and which in its revelation would cause harm to the parties of the marriage, such as the occult impediment of crime, the vicar dispenses from the impediment in the internal forum, and the fact of the dispensation is *not* to be noted in the marriage register.[51]

But if the parties of the marriage freely consent to reveal the matter to the local ordinary in the internal non-sacramental forum, or if the impediment is public in nature although occult in fact, then the fact of the granting of the dispensation by the vicar in the internal non-sacramental forum is to be noted in the secret archives of the diocese.[52] When the secret which is occult in fact, though it be public of its nature, must be kept from the local ordinary, the fact that a dispensation was granted by the substitute is to be recorded in the register of the Sacred Penitentiary.[53]

ARTICLE 2. THE SUBSTITUTE'S POWER TO DELEGATE

It has already been demonstrated that the substitute vicar holds an ecclesiastical office in the proper and strict sense.[54] It follows, then, that within the limits of his jurisdiction, and according to the norms given in the general law, the vicar can delegate some other priest either for a

---

49 Cf. O'Keeffe, *Matrimonial Dispensations*, p. 156.

50 Cf. Brennan, *Simple Convalidation of Marriage*, p. 105.

51 Cf. Cappello, *De Matrimonio*, n. 236.

52 Cf. O'Rourke, *Parish Registers*, p. 76.

53 Cf. Cappello, *loc. cit.*

54 Cf. *supra*, pp. 11 ff.

particular case or for all cases alike in the matter of granting dispensations from matrimonial impediments in the circumstances which warrant the vicar's own action.[55] There likewise can be no question of the vicar's competence to delegate another priest to assist at a particular marriage, or to delegate an assistant priest of the parish to assist at all marriages within the parish.[56]

In giving this latter delegation, however, the vicar must abide by the general rules which are stated in canon 1096. Thus the power to assist at any and all marriages within the parish can be validly delegated only to an assistant priest of the parish. If, for assistance at marriage a vicar is to delegate a priest who is not an assistant of the parish, then three things are required. First, the delegation can be given only to a priest. But it does not matter whether the priest be approved for exercising the care of souls or for the hearing of confessions within the diocese. Secondly, the delegation must be given to a specified priest, who is named either explicitly or implicity, directly or indirectly. Thirdly, the delegation must be given for a specified marriage or for specified marriages.[57]

A difficulty may sometimes arise, however, when the substitute is taking the place of a pastor who is unaccustomed to delegate his assistants with reference to assistance at any and all marriages to be celebrated in the parish or with relation to the granting of matrimonial dispensations within the measure of his own faculties. Must the vicar abide by the same rule? From the purely legal standpoint it cannot be denied that even in such circumstances the

[55] Can. 199, § 1. Cf. Claeys-Boúúaert, "De Vicario Substituto"—*Jus Pontificium,* VII (1927), 79, ad V.

[56] Cf. Kearney, *The Principles of Delegation,* The Catholic University of America Canon Law Studies, n. 55 (Washington, D.C.: The Catholic University of America, 1929), pp. 76ff.; Cappello, *De Matrimonio,* n. 673.

[57] Cf. Cappello, *De Matrimonio,* n. 674.

vicar can give this general delegation. Nowhere does the law state that such delegation would be invalid.[58] But it is surely indicated as a more prudent policy for the substitute to follow the example of the pastor. The pastor's consistent refusal to delegate his assistants might possibly be founded on the general desire of the people to be married by their pastor, or on some other sufficient reason.

ARTICLE 3. OTHER RIGHTS AND DUTIES IN REGARD TO MARRIAGE.

According to canon 1097, § 1, 1°, a pastor, and for the present consideration the substitute vicar, cannot lawfully assist at a marriage unless he is morally certain that the parties are free to marry. Since the vicar will not know the parishioners as well as their pastor does, he must of necessity acquire this moral certitude from one or more of the four means at his disposal: questions put directly to the parties themselves, evidence furnished by documents, results obtained from the publication of the banns, and testimony given under oath by reliable witnesses or the parties themselves.

Though he be morally certain that the parties are free to marry, the vicar is nevertheless obliged to see that the banns of matrimony are published.[59] He may fulfill this obligation personally or through a delegate. Since the publication of the banns is prescribed for the sake of averting invalid marriages, the law regarding the publication exists as a norm to safeguard the faithful against a common danger. In view of this fact, the law also calls for observance when such a danger is not present in some particular instance.[60] In consequence of this, the banns must be pro-

---

58 Cf. can. 11.

59 Can. 1022.

60 Cf. can. 21.

claimed unless the local ordinary has granted a dispensation from their publication.[61]

The additional proper pastors which the parties may have must also be notified in order that they too may publish the banns in their parishes.[62] If one of the parties has lived in one or more other places for a period of six months after attaining the age of puberty, the case must be referred to the ordinary, who will decide whether the banns should be published in each locality.[63] If, however, the ordinary prudently allows a contrary custom to exist in the diocese, such a custom may safely be followed by the vicar.[64]

Before the vicar will actually assist at a wedding he must have in his possession all the documents that are prescribed by law. These include the baptismal records of the parties, the permission to perform the marriage if such permission is needed,[65] and the necessary dispensations, if such be needed.

After the marriage has taken place the vicar must see that the fact of the marriage is recorded in the matrimonial register of the parish church.[66] Notice of the marriage must also be sent to the parishes where the parties were baptized, so that the marriage may be noted in the baptismal record there.[67]

Besides these duties which are regularly connected with the marriage ceremony, it may happen that the vicar will be asked to rectify an invalid marriage. There is no denying that zeal will prompt him to do everything possible to have

---

61 Cf. can. 1028, §§ 1, 2.

62 Cf. can. 1023, § 1; 93, §§ 1, 2, 3; 94, § 1.

63 Cf. can. 1023, § 2.

64 Cf. can. 5.

65 Cf. can. 1097, § 1, 3°.

66 Can. 1103, § 1.

67 Can. 1103, § 2.

such a marriage properly convalidated. But in this matter especially it is necessary for the vicar to proceed with the utmost caution and prudence.

It is not unlikely that the marriage in question has been brought to the attention of the regular pastor at some previous date. The pastor, knowing the parties and all the circumstances attending the case, may in the best interests of the Church and of the parties have hesitated to act. Until he has uncovered all the facts surrounding the case the vicar must not proceed to rectify the unvalid union, for to do so could imply an undue haste on his part. After he has become fully acquainted with the case, and when he can be of genuine assistance to the parties in having the marriage convalidated, then the vicar should take corresponding action in line with his pastoral responsibilities for the care of the souls who at the time must look to him for spiritual guidance.

CHAPTER VI

The Administration of the Sacraments

Canon 474 explicitly states that as long as the local ordinary or the pastor has not excepted anything from the scope of his office the substitute vicar has the same rights and duties as the pastor in matters which pertain to the care of souls. The vicar has these rights and duties in virtue of the office which he holds.[1] Claeys-Boúúaert remarks that the substitute, just like the pastor, must administer the sacraments to the faithful.[2] The precise manner in which this is to be done, as well as the performance of other duties which devolve upon the substitute by reason of his office, will constitute the material for this chapter.

Article 1. Baptism.

The ordinary minister of solemn baptism is a priest. The lawful administration of solemn baptism, however, is reserved to the bishop of the diocese or to the pastor.[3] The substitute, if legitimately appointed, is, of course, the "pastor" during the time he holds office.[4] The term *parochus* in canon 738, § 1, however, does not include any and all pastors alike; it is the proper pastor of the person

[1] Cf. *supra*, pp. 11 ff.

[2] "De Vicario Substituto"—*Jus Pontificium,* VII (1927), 80: "Generatim potest, et, ad normam juris, debet vicarius substitutus administrare sacramenta, quorum collatio parocho incumbit."

[3] Cf. can. 738, § 1.

[4] Cf. can. 451, § 2, 2°; Waldon, *The Minister of Baptism,* The Catholic University of America Canon Law Studies, n. 170 (Washington, D.C.: The Catholic University of America Press, 1942), p. 72.

to be baptized who is constituted as the lawful minister of solemn baptism.[5]

If it happen that a person has more than one proper pastor in view of the simultaneous possession of a domicile in one parish and of a quasi-domicile in another, then a choice must be made between these two pastors. If a minor is to be baptized, the choice is to be made by the parents or the guardians. If an adult is to receive the sacrament, he himself must choose the pastor who will baptize him.[6]

Before the vicar is allowed to administer baptism to an infant, the vicar must be asked to do so by the parents or the guardians of the child. The parents of a child have certain rights and prerogatives that the church has always guarded and preserved. Even in regard to this most essential sacrament the rights of the parents must be respected. Therefore the vicar would do wrong to baptize any child against the wishes of the parents. The only instance in which the wishes of the parents may be disregarded occurs when the child is in danger of death.[7] In such a case the eternal salvation of the child takes precedence over the natural rights of the parents.

If lax Catholics offer their children for baptism, the children may be baptized if there is a well-founded hope that the parents will change their way of life.[8] Should non-Catholics ask the vicar to baptize their children, the vicar may do so if the parents reliably guarantee that the children

---

[5] Cf. Waldron, *op. cit.*, p. 73; Noldin, *De Sacramentis*, n. 64; Vermeersch-Creusen, *Epitome*, II. n. 15.

[6] Cf. Waldron, *op. cit.*, pp. 74-76.

[7] Cf. cans. 750; 751.

[8] Cf. S. C. de Prop. Fide, 31 ian. 1796—*Collectanea S. Congregationis de Propaganda Fide* (Romae: Typographia Polyglotta S. C. de Propaganda Fide, 1893), n. 625 (hereafter cited Collectanea).

will receive a Catholic education.[9] When the vicar knows that the parents offer their children for baptism because of superstitious reasons [10]or with the intention of rearing their children as non-Catholics, he is obliged to refuse to administer the sacrament.[11]

If an adult [12] seeks baptism, the vicar must first verify the existence of three conditions in the subject seeking baptism. The first condition which must be present for the valid reception of baptism is the existence of the proper intention of receiving the sacrament. This intention, of course, resides in the will of the recipient of the sacrament; the vicar can only judge from external signs whether or not this intention does exist.[13] Because of his dependence on external signs the vicar will stress the necessity of having the proper intention during the course of instructions which will precede the baptism of the adult.

This series of instructions will also help the vicar to verify the existence of the second condition which is required for the fruitful reception of baptism: the knowledge of and the faith of the catechumen in the principal revealed truths of the Catholic faith.

If time permits, the vicar must give a complete course of instructions based on Catholic doctrine and practices. Even if the person is dying, the vicar must not forego instructing the prospective recipient concerning the existence of God and His remunerative justice, the doctrine of the Trinity and of the Incarnation. The vicar must also secure

---

[9] Cf. can. 750, § 2.

[10] Cf. Vermeersch-Creusen, *Epitome,* II. n. 33.

[11] Cf. can. 750, § 2.

[12] Cf. can. 745, § 2, 2°.

[13] Cf. Waldron, *The Minister of Baptism,* pp. 80-88.

an act of faith in these dogmas from the dying person if at all possible.[14]

The third condition that must be present in the one who is to receive baptism is sorrow for sins. This sorrow must extend, in a general way, to all past sins, but particularly to past grievous sins. A habitual sorrow suffices [15] for the fruitful reception of this sacrament.[16]

When the vicar deems an adult to be sufficiently prepared to receive baptism, he should proceed to administer the sacrament. The precise manner in which this will be done will depend upon the category into which the subject of baptism falls. One of two possibilities will occur: 1) when the person is to be baptized absolutely, no other formalities are required save the actual administration of baptism; and 2) when the adult is to be baptized conditionally, the following order must be observed: the abjuration of heresy or the profession of faith made before two witnesses [17] will precede the conditional conferring of the baptism and the hearing of the confession which is followed by conditional absolution. If the party to be received into the Church is already validly baptized, the vicar merely receives the profession of faith and thereupon absolves from the censure before he imparts sacramental absolution from the sins.[18]

After the sacrament has been administered the vicar must record in the special baptismal register of the parish the name of each person he baptized. It is also prescribed that

---

[14] Cf. S. C. S. Off. (Quebec), 25 ian. 1703—*Fontes*, n. 764. Cf. also Connell, "Priestly Ministry of the Essentials of Faith"—*ER*, LXXVI (1927), 570 ff.

[15] Cf. can. 752, § 1; Noldin, *De Sacramentis*, n. 73.

[16] Cf. Waldron, *The Minister of Baptism*, p. 90; Noldin, *loc. cit.*

[17] Cf. can. 2314, § 2; Waldron, *The Minister of Baptism*, pp. 93 ff.

[18] Cf. S. C. S. Off., 20 iul. 1859—*Fontes*, n. 953.

the name of the minister be recorded, together with the names of the parents and of the god-parents. The day and the place of the conferring of the sacrament are also to be noted in the baptismal register.[19]

ARTICLE 2. CONFIRMATION.[20]

While it is difficult to determine the exact time in history when simple priests were accredited with the right to confirm, it is known that as early as the fourth century the priests of Egypt administered confirmation whenever the bishop was absent from the diocese.[21] In the Western Church the Spanish priests of the fifth century also had the right to confirm their subjects in the absence of the bishop and also whenever the bishop commanded them to do so.[22]

From this time onward the practice on the part of simple priests to confer confirmation was gradually extended throughout the whole of the Eastern Church. In the Western Church, however, the practice was slowly restricted until the faculty of confirming was enjoyed by simple priests only in the most extraordinary circumstances.[23]

---

19 Cf. can. 777, § 1. Cf. also O'Rourke, *Parish Registers,* The Catholic University of America Canon Law Studies, n. 88 (Washington, D.C.: The Catholic University of America, 1934), pp. 46 ff.

20 For a substantially complete historico-canonical treatment regarding the minister of this sacrament, cf. Coleman, *The Minister of Confirmation,* The Catholic University of America Canon Law Studies, n. 125 (Washington, D.C.: The Catholic University of America Press, 1941).

21 Cf. Ambrosiaster, *Commentaria in Epistolam ad Ephesios—MPG,* XVII, 388.

22 I Provincial Council of Toledo (400), can. 20: " Episcopo sane certum est omni tempore licere chrisma conficere: sine conscientia autem episcopi, nihil penitus faciendum; statutum vero est, diaconem non chrismare, sed presbyterum absente episcopo, presente vero si ab ipso fuerit praeceptum." Harduin, I, 992, ad can. XX. Cf. Coleman, *The Minister of Confirmation,* pp. 22 ff.

23 Cf. Coleman, *The Minister of Confirmation,* pp. 31-35.

In 1929, however, the ordinaries of China were granted the extraordinary faculty from the Holy See which allowed them to give all their priests permission to administer confirmation to infants and adults alike, in danger of death. This faculty could be used even in the episcopal city, as long as the bishop could not be present personally to administer the sacrament.[24]

On September 14, 1946, the Sacred Congregation of the Sacraments issued a decree, effective January 1, 1947, which in a sense is an extension of the Chinese indult. By apostolic decree the faculty of confirming as extraordinary ministers is given a) to pastors who govern a particular territory; b) to vicars who rule a parish in the name of a moral person in whom the title of pastor is vested and to vicars who are administrators in juridically vacant parishes; and c) to priests to whom is entrusted with exclusiveness and stability the care of souls within a definite territory and for a definite church when they function like pastors with all the pastoral rights and duties incumbent on them.[25]

At first reading it could seem that the substitute vicar is included as one who can validly and lawfully administer the Sacrament of confirmation, since the vicar is equivalent to a pastor in law, according to the norms of canon 451, § 2, and the terms of the rescript may seem to demand a wide interpretation.[26]

But upon close examination of the text of the indult it is seen that the words "*iisdem dumtaxat*" are used to designate with exclusiveness the priests who have been given the

---

[24] Primum Concilium Sinense (Zi-Ka-Wei: Typographia Missionis Catholicae, 1929), n. 273. Cf. *AAS,* XXVII (1935), 13 for faculties given to priests of South America.

[25] *AAS,* XXXVIII (1946), 352 ff.

[26] Cf. can. 50.

faculty to confirm. If the term *pastor* were used to denote all those priests who have an equivalent pastoral status according to the norms of canon 451, § 2, then the divisions b) and c) in the classification would appear useless,[27] since the priests listed under these categories are pastors in the sense of canon 451, § 2. The wording of the decree, therefore, would have to be considered faulty, for it would have been sufficient for the decree to state that "all those who are pastors in the sense of canon 451, § 2, are given the faculty to confirm."

Since the decree mentions three distinct classes of priests and refers to "*iisdem dumtaxat*" as having the right and the obligation to confirm their subjects under certain and specified conditions, it must be inferred that all others are to be excluded.[28] The substitute vicar, therefore, even though he is taking the place of the pastor in all matters which pertain to the care of souls, does not possess the faculty to administer confirmation, since he is not a pastor in the sense understood by the decree nor is he one of the vicars mentioned by name.

Except in the extraordinary case noted above, the ordinary minister of the sacrament of confirmation is the bishop. Very rarely will it happen that a vicar will be in charge of a parish when the bishop visits it for the conferring of this sacrament. If it should happen, however, then the vicar is obliged to prepare the ones to be confirmed by instituting a course of instructions during which he will explain the nature and the effects of the sacrament of confirmation upon the soul.[29] The vicar must instruct each candidate to have a sponsor, as at baptism, unless the

---

27 Cf. *supra*, p. 84.

28 Cf. can. 49.

29 Cf. can. 786.

minister of the sacrament, for a just reason, decides otherwise.[30]

After the sacrament has been conferred the vicar will be bound to make a record of the fact in the confirmation register. He must also include mention of the name of the minister, of the names of those confirmed, of the names of the sponsors, of the day on which and of the place where the sacrament was conferred. A notation is also to be made in the baptismal register.[31] If any of the persons confirmed were from another parish, the vicar must send a notification of the fact of confirmation to that person's proper pastor.[32]

ARTICLE 3. PENANCE

It has already been shown that the vicar has ordinary jurisdiction to hear confessions within his territory.[33] This faculty to hear confessions is attached to the office that he holds, as authors generally agree.[34] Consequently by reason of his office the vicar can hear the confessions of all who come to him within the limits of the parish,[35] and he can hear the confessions of his subjects even outside the parish limits.[36]

When hearing the confessions of the faithful, however, the substitute is bound to abide by the reservation of sins

---

30 Cf. cann. 793; 794, §§ 1-2.

31 Cf. can. 798.

32 Cf. can. 799.

33 Cf. *supra*, pp. 11 ff.

34 Cf. Claeys-Boúúaert, "De Vicario Substituto"—*Jus Pontificium*, VII (1927), 80; Cappello, "De Vicario Substituto"—*Periodica*, XIX (1930), 2*.

35 Cf. cans. 873, § 1; 881, § 1.

36 Cf. can. 881, § 2.

that is made by the local ordinary,[37] as well as the one contained in the Code.[38] During the paschal season, however, the pastor and consequently also the substitute vicar [39] is permitted by the general law to absolve from all sins which the ordinary has reserved to himself [40] either in the diocesan synod or at a time when no synod was being held.[41] Confessions heard by the vicar at a time other than the paschal season are not privileged, therefore he can absolve from reserved sins only in those cases where the reservations are considered by law as having ceased for special occasions.

Canon 900 states that in the following cases all reservations of sins cease: [42] 1) whenever the vicar hears the confession of a sick person who is unable to leave the house. Probably included under the general term "sick person" are those who suffer any bodily infirmity such as broken bones and the like which confines them to the house.[43] 2) Whenever the vicar hears the confessions of spouses who confess with a view to preparing themselves for the contracting of marriage. All those who are readying themselves for marriage are included, whether or not they are formally engaged.[44] 3) Whenever the proper superior has refused to grant the faculty sought in connection with some

---

[37] Can. 893, § 1. Cf. Ayrinhac, *Legislation on the Sacraments* (London, New York, Toronto: Longmans, Green and Co., 1928), pp. 233 ff; 241 ff.

[38] Can. 894. Cf. Ayrinhac, *op. cit.*, pp. 240 ff.

[39] Cf. Ayrinhac, *op. cit.*, p. 249.

[40] Can. 899, § 3.

[41] Cf. Ayrinhac, *op. cit.*, p. 249.

[42] Since the canon makes no distinction its meaning must be extended to all reservations of sins, whether reserved to the Pope, to the local ordinary, or to a religious superior. Cf. Ayrinhac, *Legislation on the Sacraments*, pp. 249 ff; Vermeersch-Creusen, *Epitome*, II, n. 179. Cf. also P.C.I., 10 nov. 1925—*AAS*, XVII (1925), 583.

[43] Cf. Vermeersch-Creusen, *Epitome*, II, n. 179.

[44] Cf. Vermeersch-Creusen, *loc. cit.*; Ayrinhac, *loc. cit.*

determinate case. 4) Whenever, in the prudent judgment of the confessor, the faculty for absolving cannot be requested from the legitimate superior in view of serious inconvenience for the penitent or in consequence of danger of violating a secret relative to the seal of confession.

Grave inconvenience to the penitent would be present if the penitent would experience great difficulty in returning to the confessor again for absolution; if there would exist for the penitent the necessity of celebrating mass; if the need for the penitent again to present himself for confession would cause suspicion or scandal; if the penitent would find it difficult to remain in the state of sin for the period necessary to obtain the necessary faculty from the ordinary; or for other like considerations.[45]

ARTICLE 4. EXTREME UNCTION [46]

While the sacrament of extreme unction can be administered validly by any priest,[47] the ordinary minister is the pastor of the place where the sick person is staying.[48] This pastor is bound in justice to administer the sacrament. Since the substitute has the same obligations as the pastor, it must be concluded that the substitute is also bound in justice to administer this sacrament to those reasonably asking for it.[49]

---

[45] Cf. Vermeersch-Creusen, *Epitome,* II, n. 179; Ayrinhac, *Legislation on the Sacraments,* p. 250.

[46] For a complete historical and canonical treatise on this sacrament cf. Kilker, *Extreme Unction,* The Catholic University of America Canon Law Studies, n. 32 (Washington, D.C.: The Catholic University of America, 1926).

[47] Cf. can. 938, § 1.

[48] Cf. can. 938, § 2. Cf. also Kilker, *Extreme Unction,* p. 93.

[49] Excepted from the vicar's jurisdiction, though they live in the territory of the parish in which he ministers, are: 1) the diocesan bishop (can. 397, 3°); 2) the professed and the novices of a clerical religious institute, and

When administering this sacrament the vicar must follow the same norms and rules that are imposed by the law on the pastor. Thus the sacrament is to be administered only to the faithful who have reached the use of reason, and who are in danger of death from sickness or old age. All these conditions must be fulfilled for the valid administration of the sacrament.[50]

Since the state of grace is required for the fruitful reception of the sacrament,[51] the vicar should urge the sick person to make use of the sacrament of penance before receiving extreme unction. If confession is impossible inasmuch, for example, as the sick person is unconscious, the vicar can presuppose that sorrow for sins exists and he may give the sick person at least conditional absolution.[52]

Whenever the vicar doubts whether the sick person has actually attained the use of reason, whether there is an actual danger of death, or whether the person is yet alive (*homo viator*), the following norms may be of some practical value.[53]

The use of reason may be presupposed if it can be determined that the person was able to distinguish between right and wrong in at least a confused way. After the age of seven is reached this faculty is presumed to exist in a

---

also other persons who dwell day and night in the religious house by reason of employment, education, hospitality or convalescence (can. 514, § 1); 3) the members of a monastery of nuns (can. 514, § 2); 4) the members of other lay religious institutes, if a chaplain distinct from the pastor has been appointed for them (can. 514, § 3; and 5) for all those who reside at a seminary (can. 1368).

[50] Cf. Noldin, *De Sacramentis*, nn. 443 ff.; Kilker, *Extreme Unction*, pp. 123 ff.

[51] Cf. Noldin, *op. cit.*, n. 445.

[52] Cf. Noldin, *loc. cit.*

[53] Cf. can. 941.

child.[54] But like all simple legal presumptions it will give way to contrary proof.

If the vicar is called to the bedside of an insane person, extreme unction may be conditionally administered if the person gave any indication at all during his life that he could distinguish between right and wrong. Since that is usually the case, it will be rarely when the vicar will not be able to administer the sacrament at least conditionally to even the insane.[55]

What should the vicar do if he is in doubt whether the sick person is in actual danger of death either from sickness or from old age? If a physician is present the vicar should ask the expert for an opinion. It can easily happen, however, that in such a case an expert cannot determine the exact seriousness of the illness. In this, as in similar cases when a person is afflicted with a lingering disease such as cancer, consumption, and the like, the sacrament is to be conditionally administered if the vicar cannot be certain that there is actual danger of death.[56]

If the one who is anointed conditionally later definitely and absolutely is in danger of death, the vicar should repeat the administration of the sacrament conditionally. A case of this nature could occur if the vicar had anointed a person *sub conditione* before an operation inasmuch as he doubted whether there was present at the time an actual danger of death from sickness. If after the operation the person has a relapse and is in definite danger of death, the person should then again be anointed conditionally.[57]

Since the sacraments were instituted for the use of the living, the vicar may be undecided what procedure to follow

---

[54] Cf. can. 88, § 3.

[55] Cf. Kilker, *Extreme Unction*, p. 208.

[56] Cf. Kilker, *op. cit.*, p. 209.

[57] Cf. Kilker, *loc. cit.*

if he arrives at a home or on the scene of an accident only to find that the person he came to anoint has none of the usual signs of life. When such circumstances exist the vicar must remember that it is impossible to determine by sight and touch alone the exact moment when death actually takes place.[58] Since this is true, the vicar may, in practice, administer extreme unction conditionally even after apparent death, such as occurs when the heart has stopped beating, when no pulse-beat is discernible, and the like.

How long after apparent death has set in may the vicar administer the sacrament? Various time limits are indicated by the authors. If the person has suffered from a long illness, the vicar may safely anoint a person conditionally for at least a half hour after apparent death.[59] In cases of sudden death the time limit set by the authors varies from one hour [60] to two hours [61] and more. Kilker (1901-1944) stated: " In practice a priest is amply justified in anointing a man supposedly dead (from a sudden and unexpected cause) up until the time when advanced decomposition has set in. This period may last for many hours and even thru several entire days, depending of course, upon the rapidity with which the putrefaction occurs." [62]

When the vicar conditionally anoints a sick person, with what condition should he invest his administration of the sacrament? Authors claim that the formulated condition should be "*si capax es*" or "*si vivis*" but never "*si dispositus es.*" The reason is obvious. If the last named condition were set and the sick person were actually not

[58] Cf. Kilker, *Extreme Unction*, pp. 210 ff.

[59] Cf. Noldin, *De Sacramentis*, n. 296; Kilker, *op. cit.*, p. 218.

[60] Cf. Vermeersch-Creusen, *Epitome*, II, n. 225.

[61] Cf. Noldin, *loc. cit.*

[62] *Extreme Unction*, p. 219.

disposed, then no effects of the sacrament could follow; in a word the sacrament would not be conferred. If the first named conditions were set by the vicar and the person were capable of being validly anointed, then the sacrament would be conferred. Inasmuch as the sick person thus could validly receive the sacrament, the subsequent removal of any obstacle or hindrance which prevented the fruitful reception of the sacrament at the time of its administration would bring about the revival of the effects of the sacrament for the one who previously received the sacrament validly.[63]

While canon 942 instructs the minister of this sacrament not to confer the sacrament on those who are impenitent or who contumaciously persevere in manifest mortal sin, it also states that, if there is any doubt concerning these conditions, the sacrament is to be administered conditionally. The condition to be used even in such circumstances is not "*si non es impoenitens,*" but rather "*si capax es.*" The reason for this, as Noldin explains, lies in the fact that because of the probable impenitence of the one receiving the sacrament there is doubt concerning the person's intention of receiving the sacrament, which intention is necessary for the validity of the sacrament. The doubt on which the condition is based, therefore, is not extended to his disposition which is required for the fruitful reception of this sacrament.[64]

ARTICLE 5. PREACHING AND CATECHETICAL INSTRUCTION

A. In the Church.

By the very fact that the vicar is taking the place of the pastor, the obligation of preaching to the people devolves upon him. In virtue of canon 1347 the vicar has the

[63] Cf. Noldin, *De Sacramentis,* n. 446; Kilker, *Extreme Unction,* p. 245.

[64] Cf. Noldin, *De Sacramentis,* n. 446; Vermeersch-Creusen, *Epitome,* II, n. 226; Davis, *Moral and Pastoral Theology,* IV, pp. 8 ff.

obligation of making known to the people the truths which they must accept and the actions they are obliged to perform in order that they may gain eternal salvation.

The time and manner of fulfilling this obligation is specified in canon 1344. On each Sunday and day of precept the vicar must deliver a homily to the people. It is recommended that this homily be given during the Mass at which the majority of the parishioners attends. For a just cause the ordinary may permit the homily to be omitted on some of the prescribed days.

In addition to the homily the vicar is likewise commanded to explain the catechism to the adult members of the congregation on Sundays and holydays of obligation.[65] It is to be noted that the hour when this instruction is to be given is not determined by the general law. Therefore it could be given at any time the pastor or vicar chooses.[66] If the majority of the people would have to miss this instruction if it were given at an inconvenient time or for the reason that the people live far from the church, the vicar is certainly permitted to have this instruction at the time of the parish mass.

It seems permitted, too, to combine the homily and the catechetical instruction in one sermon. Although the authors are silent on this question, there seems to be no reasonable objection against satisfying both obligations with the one act.[67]

---

[65] Can. 1332.

[66] Cf. Jansen, *Canonical Provisions for Catechetical Instruction,* The Catholic University of America Canon Law Studies, n. 107 (Washington, D.C.: The Catholic University of America, 1937), p. 100 (hereafter cited *Catechetical Instruction*).

[67] Jansen (*Catechetical Instruction,* p. 101) suggests that the conflict could be solved " by having both a short well prepared instruction and a sermon." But it appears that if the two obligations can be solved by means of two acts in close succession, then there is no reason why they cannot be fulfilled by means of one act which includes the necessary elements of a homily and of a catechetical instruction.

The III Plenary Council of Baltimore (1884) decreed that the sermon is to be accommodated to the intelligence of the hearers. And the Council also commanded that a five minute sermon be preached at every mass, even the very early ones, on every Sunday and solemn feast, the summer time not excepted.[68] This decree which refers more to a catechetical instruction than to a sermon in the strict sense, is not contrary to the law of canon 1345. Consequently this provision of the Council must still be observed in the United States.

If a regular schedule of sermons has been ordered by the ordinary of the place, the provisions of the III Plenary Council of Baltimore will nevertheless have to be observed.[69] The sermon and the catechetical instruction can be combined, however, as was previously explained.

B. In the School

Canon 1329 states that one of the most grave and serious duties of the pastor is to provide for the religious instruction of his parishioners. The pastor is urged to fulfill this obligation with special zeal and diligence in the case of children.[70] The duty of the pastor, and of all who take his place, with reference to catechetical instruction to the children are defined in canons 1330 and 1331.

The first duty of the vicar, as outlined in the canons here cited, is to prepare the children of the parish for the reception of the sacraments of penance, confirmation and first Holy Communion. The vicar should prepare the children by means of a special course of instructions which do not take the place of, but are added to, the regular instructions given in the parish.[71]

---

68 *Acta et Decreta Concilii Plen. Balt. III*, n. 216.

69 Cf. can. 82.

70 Cf. can. 467, § 1.

71 Cf. Jansen, *Catechetical Instruction*, p. 93.

Canon 1330 does not insist on a separate course of instructions for each of the sacraments enumerated. It does require, however, that the instructions should last for several days, and that they be given at stated times during the year. The canon evidently wants the vicar to follow the diocesan regulations, which should determine the times when the instructions are to be given.[72]

The series of instructions which precede first Holy Communion, however, should be given during the Lenten season.[73] Any reasonable cause will be sufficient for the vicar to choose a different time. This is evident from the words used in canon 1330, § 2°, "*si nihil obsit.*"

Particular laws in force in the United States regulate more in detail the instructions that are to precede first Holy Communion. The III Plenary Council of Baltimore (1884) decreed that the instructions are to be given three times a week for a period of six weeks prior to first Holy Communion. These instructions are to be given at the parish church or at some filial church which the children can easily attend. This decree is in no way contrary to the general law of the Church. Consequently it must still be observed in this country.[74]

After the children have received their first Holy Communion they are not to be neglected by the pastor. He still has the obligation of continuing to instruct them. Just how long the instructions will have to continue after first Holy Communion will be determined by particular law or custom.[75]

---

72 Cf. Jansen, *loc. cit.*

73 Cf. can. 1330, 2°.

74 *Acta et Decreta Concilii Plen. Balt. III,* n. 218.

75 Cf. Jansen, *Catechetical Instruction,* pp. 78 ff.

C. In General

Besides the general precepts of preaching and catechizing both the adult and the youthful members of the parish, the pastor has the special obligation of imparting specific instructions to his flock. This obligation could scarcely be imposed upon the vicar substitute who takes the place of a pastor for a short time. But if the substitute takes the pastor's place for a long period of time, he will be obliged to see that the parishioners receive these special instructions.

For the sake of completeness the specific instructions which the vicar is obliged to impart to the members of the parish will here be mentioned. The vicar must warn the faithful of the danger of reading perverse literature, especially of reading prohibited books.[76] The faithful, and especially doctors, nurses and mid-wives should be instructed in the proper manner of administering the sacrament of baptism.[77] The vicar must warn the faithful that they have a grave obligation to have their children baptized as promptly as possible.[78] The faithful should be exhorted to attend Mass and to receive Holy Communion frequently, and to make frequent visits to the Blessed Sacrament.[79]

The members of the parish should receive instructions on the nature of the sacrament of matrimony and on matrimonial impediments.[80] When members of the parish are about to be married they have a special right to be instructed concerning the sanctity of the sacrament, their mutual rights and obligations, and especially concerning the obligations of parents toward their children.[81]

---

[76] Cf. can. 1405, § 2.

[77] Cf. can. 743.

[78] Cf. can. 770.

[79] Cf. can. 1273.

[80] Cf. can. 1018.

[81] Cf. can. 1033.

CHAPTER VII

THE SUPPLYING PRIEST

The supplying priest is the one who takes the place of a pastor who will be absent from his parish for less than a week.[1] This priest is appointed to take care of the needs of the parishioners if otherwise they would be left without the proper pastoral care.

The actual appointment of the supplying priest, the circumstances surrounding his appointment, and his status after the appointment have already been discussed in Chapters I and II of this treatise.[2] There it was noted that the supplying priest does not hold an ecclesiastical office in the proper canonical sense, that he does not possess ordinary power, and that he cannot be considered as one who is delegated by the law to perform certain acts. This particular status of the supplying priest follows from a study of canon 465, § 6, which states that the pastor must provide for the needs of the faithful even when he is absent from the parish for less than a week. It must be concluded, then, that the supplying priest possesses only that power which is given to him by the pastor or by the ordinary.

Since the pastor possesses ordinary power of jurisdiction, he can delegate his power to the supplying priest wholly or in part, as he sees fit, unless the law expressly states otherwise.[3] It could be doubted, however, whether the pastor is able to grant this priest a universal delegation to take care

---

1 Cf. can. 465, § 6.

2 Cf. *supra*, pp. 16 ff.

3 Cf. can. 199, § 1.

of all matters (*ad universitatem negotiorum*).[4] But upon close examination of the law it is seen that no general restriction is placed upon the pastor's right to grant universal delegation as long as the one delegated is fit and worthy to fulfill the duties for which he is delegated.[5] Consequently, if the pastor tells the supplying priest that he has full charge of the parish with all the faculties necessary to take care of the needs of the faithful, then the delegated power which the supplying priest has thus received is to be considered as a universal delegation, insofar as the law permits.[6]

If the pastor so desires, however, he may specify the acts for which he is giving the priest authorization. Thus the pastor may instruct the priest to take care of all baptisms. Or he may delegate the supplying priest to dispense in particular cases from the law of fast and abstinence, or from the precept of hearing Mass on Sundays and holydays.[7] In no case, however, can the pastor validly delegate the supplying priest for the hearing of confessions of the faithful.[8] Nor, in all probability, can the pastor give the supplying priest a universal delegation to assist at all marriages to be celebrated in the parish during the pastor's

---

[4] Kearney (*The Principles of Delegation*, p. 76) states: "Delegation is universal when it extends to at least a general class of acts which are within the power of the delegator . . . Universal delegation implies a relation to quantity, or to the number of cases to which it extends; it is conceivable although restrictions have been made with regard to time, place or any other circumstance." Coronata (*Institutiones*, I, p. 343) defines delegation *ad universitatem causarum:* ". . . universalitas causarum censetur haberi sive tota Ordinarii iurisdictio delegatur sive aliqua tantummodo negotiorum species."

[5] Cf. Kearney, *op. cit.*, p. 91; Coronata. *Institutiones*, I, n. 288, 2°.

[6] Cf. Cappello, *Summa*, II, n. 556.

[7] Cf. can. 1245, § 1.

[8] Cf. P.C.I., 16 oct. 1919—*AAS*, XI (1919), 477.

absence. The contrary opinion, however, is held by some authors.

Coronata, for instance, believes that the pastor can give the supplying priest a universal delegation to assist at all such marriages. As a preliminary to this conclusion Coronata states that the rule of canon 1096, § 1, is not applicable in the case of a supplying priest who has a universal delegation to care for the souls of the parish. He claims that even though canon 1096, § 1, rules that a valid universal delegation to assist at marriages can be given only to assistants, the pastor can, nevertheless, so delegate a supplying priest.

He reasons that the canon in question does not prohibit a universal delegation which includes also the general faculty to assist at marriages, but that the canon prohibits a general delegation to assist at marriages only when the universal care of souls is not at the same time delegated.[9]

The reasoning behind Coronata's conclusion seems to be specious. No one doubts that the lawgiver, if he had so desired, could have made a universal delegation to assist at marriages associable with the delegation whereby the universal care of souls is committed. But when the law is clear in itself, we are forbidden to have recourse to the mind of the legislator in order to uphold an opinion.[10] And in this case the law is clear.[11]

When the law states "*exclusis quibuslibet delegationibus,*" there can be no mistaking the meaning of the words; the granting of a general delegation is without any dis-

---

[9] Coronata, *Institutiones,* I, 576, footnote 7.

[10] Cf. can. 18.

[11] Canon 1096, 1: Licentia assistendi matrimonio concessa ad normam 1095, § 2, [a parocho vel ordinario loci infra fines sui territorii] dari expresse debet sacerdoti determinato ad matrimonium determinatum, exclusis quibuslibet delegationibus generalibus, nisi agatur de vicariis cooperatoribus pro paroecia cui addicti sunt; secus irrita est.

tinction precluded except when it is done in favor of parochial assistant priests with special relation to the marriages celebrated in the parish where they are assigned.

It seems, therefore, that the pastor cannot validly grant to the supplying priest a universal delegation to assist at all marriages in the parish. The pastor seems rather under the necessity of giving the priest a specific delegation for each marriage at which he desires the supplying priest to assist.[12] Accordingly it appears that the supplying priest cannot validly assist at the marriage either of parishioners or of non-parishioners when the pastor has no knowledge of the proposed celebration of the marriage, and in consequence could not have granted a specific delegation for assistance at the marriage.

It should be remembered, however, that the pastor has ordinary power to dispense from quite a number of the matrimonial impediments and also from the juridically required form of marriage in cases wherein the parties are beset by the danger of death. The pastor also possesses ordinary power to dispense from ecclesiastical impediments in occult cases when all things are prepared for a wedding.[13] Therefore the pastor, if he so desires, may delegate this power to the supplying priest.[14]

Since the supplying priest is taking the place of the pastor, he will be obliged to administer the other sacraments to the faithful who legitimately ask for them, and to render this service in accordance with the instructions he has received from the pastor. Thus he will be obliged to administer baptism to all who have a right to be baptized at the parish. The supplying priest must also celebrate mass

---

[12] Cf. Cappello, *De Matrimonio*, n. 650.

[13] Cf. cans. 1044; 1045.

[14] Cf. can. 199. Cf. also Cappello, *De Matrimonio*, n. 234.

for the people at the usual time, and he is obliged to administer Holy Communion to them.

If any of the parishioners are dangerously sick, the supplying priest is expected to administer to them the last rites of the Church. Holy Viaticum must be taken to the sick who are in danger of death, and It may be administered as often as their confessor allows them to receive on successive days.[15]

Since the supplying priest does not have ordinary jurisdiction for the hearing of confessions, the pastor must, if the priest does not already possess a delegated jurisdiction, present his name to the bishop, who will then grant the needed delegated jurisdiction for the hearing of confessions. Naturally, if the supplying priest enjoys the possession of the diocesan faculties, then no further act of delegation for the hearing of confessions is needed. If the one taking the place of the pastor is a religious, then at least the presumed permission of the religious superior is postulated for the lawful use of this delegated jurisdiction.[16]

When the pastor is absent from the parish over a Sunday or a Holyday, the supplying priest should preach to the people and give a catechetical instruction.[17]

In all these matters, however, the supplying priest must keep in mind that the scope of his duties depends on the will of the pastor. Consequently the pastor may limit or increase the list of duties outlined above, always bearing in mind, however, the fact that the general law may not be contravened either by the pastor or by the priest who supplies the pastoral service for him.

---

[15] Cf. can. 864, § 3.

[16] Cf. can. 874, § 1.

[17] Cf. cans. 1332, 1334. Cf. also *Acta et Decreta Concilii Plen. Balt. III*, n. 216.

CONCLUSIONS

1. Prior to the present Code of Canon Law the duties of the substitute vicar were fulfilled by the temporary vicar.

2. A substitute vicar cannot be appointed if the pastor will be absent from his parish for less than seven days.

3. In a case of unforeseen and urgent absence, a pastor validly appoints a substitute even though the pastor neglects to notify the ordinary of the appointment.

4. The substitute vicar holds an ecclesiastical office in the strict sense. Consequently he possesses ordinary power to care for the needs of the parishioners committed to his charge.

5. The substitute vicar may delegate another priest to assist him in discharging his pastoral office in the same way as the pastor can do so.

6. The substitute acts invalidly if he acts contrary to the restrictions imposed on him by the pastor or the ordinary.

7. The substitute is not given charge of the temporal administration of the parish.

8. In cases of doubt the substitute is not obliged to celebrate the *missa pro populo*.

9. The substitute vicar has not been granted the faculty of administering the sacrament of Confirmation in the recent decree (September 14, 1946) of the Sacred Congregation of the Sacraments.

10. The supplying priest does not possess an ecclesiastical office in the strict sense, nor does he possess any ordinary power in view of being constituted as a supplying priest.

11. The supplying priest must abide by the mandate of the pastor.

BIBLIOGRAPHY

Sources

Acta Apostolicae Sedis, Commentarium Officiale, Romae, 1909—

Acta et Decreta Concilii Plenarii Americae Latinae in Urbe Celebrati, A. D. MDCCCXCIX, Romae: Typis Polyglottis Vaticanis, 1902.

Acta et Decreta Concilii Plenarii Baltimorensis Tertii, A. D..... MDCCCLXXXIV, Baltimorae: John Murphy, 1886.

Acta et Decreta Sacrorum Conciliorum Recentiorum, Collectio Lacensis, 7 vols., Friburgi Brisgoviae, 1870-1890.

Acta Sanctae Sedis, 41 vols., Romae, 1865-1908.

Canones et Decreta Sacrosancti Oecumenici Concilii Tridentini, Editio novissima ad Fidem Optimorum Exemplarium Castigate Impressa (XIX reimpressio stereotypa), Taurini, 1913.

Codex Iuris Canonici Pii X Pontificis Maximi iussu digestus Benedicti Papae XV auctoritate promulgatus, Romae: Typis Polyglottis Vaticanis, 1917; Reimpressio, 1919.

Codicis Iuris Canonici Fontes, cura Emi Petri Card. Gasparri editi, 9 vols. Romae (postea Civitate Vaticana): Typis Polyglottis Vaticanis, 1923-1939. (Vols. VII-IX, ed cura et studio Emi Iustiniani Serédi).

Collectanea S. Congregationis de Propaganda Fide, Romae: Typographia Polyglotta S. C. de Propaganda Fide, 1893.

Collectanea S. Congregationis de Propaganda Fide, 2 vols., Romae: Typographia Polyglotta S. C. de Propaganda Fide, 1907.

Corpus Iuris Canonici, Editio Lipsiensis II (Richter-Friedberg), 2 vols., Lipsiae, 1879-1881.

Hardouin, J., *Conciliorum Collectio Regia Maxima,* 12 vols., Parisiis, 1714-1715.

Jaffé, p., *Regesta Pontificium Romanorum ab condita Ecclesia ad annum post Christum natum MCXCVIII,* 2 ed., cura Wattenbach, Kaltenbrunner (ad annum 590), Ewald (anno 590-882), Löwenfeld (anno 882-1198), 2 vols., Lipsiae, 1885-1888.

Labbeus, P., et Cossartius, G., *Sacrorum Conciliorum Nova et Amplissima Collectio,* 17 vols., Florentiae, 1759-1774.

Mansi, J, *Sacrorum Conciliorum Nova et Amplissima Collectio,* 53 vols. in 60, Paris-Anhern-Leipzig, 1901-1927.

Pallottini, Salvator, *Collectio Omnium Conclusionum et Resolutionum Quae in Causis Propositis apud Sacram Congregationem Cardinalium S. Concilii Tridentini Interpretum Prodierunt ab eius Institutione anno MDLXIV ad annum MDCCCLX, distinctis titulis alphebetico ordine per materias digesta,* 18 vols., Romae, 1868-1893.

Pius VI, *Responsio ad Metropolitanas Moguntinum, Trevirensem, Coloniensem, Salisburgensem super Nunciaturis Apostolicis,* Romae, 1789.

Thesaurus Resolutionum Sacrae Congregationis Concilii, 167 vols., Romae, 1718-1908.

AUTHORS

Ayrinhac, H. A., *Constitution of the Church,* London, New York, Toronto: Longmans, Green and Co., 1930.

————, Legislation on the Sacraments, London, New York, Toronto: Longmans, Green and Co., 1928.

Barbosa, A., *Collectanea Doctorum in Ius Pontificium,* Lugduni, 1632.

————, *Iuris Ecclesiastici Universi Libri Tres,* Lugduni, 1660.

Beste, U., *Introductio in Codicem,* ed. altera, Collegeville, Minn.: St. John's Abbey Press, 1944.

Bouix, D., *Tractus de Parocho,* 3 ed., Parisiis, 1880.

Bouscaren, T. L., *The Canon Law Digest,* 2 vols., Milwaukee: Bruce Publishing Co., 1934-1943.

Boyle, D., *The Juridic Effect of Moral Certitude on Pre-Nuptial Guarantees,* The Catholic University of America Canon Law Studies, n. 150, Washington, D.C.: The Catholic University of America Press, 1942.

Canavan, W., *Profession of Faith,* The Catholic University of America Canon Law Studies, n. 151, Washington, D.C.: The Catholic University of America Press, 1942.

Cappello, F., *Summa Iuris Canonici,* 3 vols., Taurini: Marietti, Vol. I, 3 ed., 1938; Vol. II, 1930.

————, *Tractatus Canonico-Moralis de Sacramentis,* 3 vols., Vol. III, De Matrimonio, 3 ed., Taurini: Marietti, 1933.

Chelodi, J.—Bertagnolli, E., *Ius de Personis,* ed. altera, Trento: Ardesi, 1927.

Coleman. J., *The Minister of Confirmation,* The Catholic University of America Canon Law Studies, n. 125, Washington, D.C.: The Catholic University of America Press, 1941.

Coronata, Matthaeus, Conte A. *Institutiones Iuris Canonici,* 5 vols., Vol. I, ed. altera, Taurini: Marietti, 1939.

Davis, H., *Moral and Pastoral Theology,* 3 ed., 4 vols., London: Sheed and Ward, 1938.

De Meester, A., *Juris Canonici et Juris Canonico-civilis Compendium,* 3 vols. in 4, Brugis: 1921-1928.

Donnellan, T., *The Obligation of the* MISSA PRO POPULO, The Catholic University of America Canon Law Studies, n. 155, Washington, D.C., The Catholic University of America Press, 1942.

Fanfani, L., *De Iure Parochorum,* Taurini, Romae: Marietti, 1924.

Ferraris, F. L., *Prompta Bibliotheca Canonica, Iuridica, Moralis, Theologica, necnon Ascetica, Polemica, Rubricistica, Historica,* ed. noviss., 9 vols., Romae, 1885-1899.

Ferry, W., *Stole Fees,* The Catholic University of America Canon Law Studies, n. 59, Washington, D.C.: The Catholic University of America, 1930.

Forcellini, A, *Totius Latinitatis Lexicon,* 6 vols., Prati: Typis Aldinianis, 1858-1860.

Jansen, R., *Canonical Provisions for Catechetical Instruction,* The Catholic University of America Canon Law Studies, n. 107, Washington, D.C.: The Catholic University of America, 1937.

Kearney, R., *The Principles of Delegation,* The Catholic University of America Canon Law Studies, n. 55, Washington, D. C.: The Catholic University of America, 1929.

Kilker, A., *Extreme Unction,* The Catholic University of America Canon Law Studies, n. 32, Washington, D.C.: The Catholic University of America, 1926.

Laurentius, Iosephus, *Institutiones Iuris Ecclesiastici,* ed. altera, Friburgi: Herder, 1908.

Lehmkuhl, A., *Theologia Moralis,* 11. ed., 2 vols., Friburgi Brisgoviae, 1910.

McBride, J. T., *The Incardination and Excardination of Seculars,* The Catholic University of America Canon Law Studies, n. 145, Washington, D.C.: The Catholic University of America Press, 1941.

Meier, C., *Penal Administrative Procedure Against Negligent Pastors,* The Catholic University of America Canon Law Studies, n. 140, Washington, D.C.: The Catholic University of America Press, 1941.

Migne, J. *Patrologiae Cursus Completus, Series Graeca,* 161 vols., Parisiis, 1856-1866.

Motry, L., *Diocesan Faculties According to the Code of Canon Law,* The Catholic University of America Canon Law Studies, n. 16, Washington, D.C.: The Catholic University of America, 1923.

Noldin, H., *Summa Theologiae Moralis iuxta Codicem Iuris Canonici Scholarum Usui Accommodavit A. Schmitt,* 3 vols., Vol. III, 25 ed., Oeniponte: Rauch, 1938.

O'Keeffe, G., *Matrimonial Dispensations, Powers of Bishops, Priests, and Confessors,* The Catholic University of America Canon Law Studies, n. 45, Washington, D.C.: The Catholic University of America, 1927.

Ojetti, B., *Synopsis Rerum Moralium et Iuris Pontificii,* 3. ed., 3 vols. and Index, Romae, 1909-1914.

O'Rourke, J., *Parish Registers,* The Catholic University of America Canon Law Studies, n. 88, Washington, D.C.: The Catholic University of America, 1934.

Pirhing, E., *Jus Canonicum Nova Methodo Explicatum,* 5 vols. in 4, Dilingae, 1674-1678.

Ramstein, M., *The Pastor and Marriage Cases,* 2 ed., New York: Benziger Bros., 1938.

Raus, J. B., *Institutiones Canonicae,* 2 ed., Vitte: Parisii, 1931.

Reiffenstuel, A., *Jus Canonicum Universum,* 5 vols. in 7, Parisiis, 1735.

Santi, F., *Praelectiones Iuris Canonici,* 2 vols., Ratisbonae, Neo-Eboraci, Cincinnati, 1886.

Schmalzgrueber, F., *Jus Ecclesiasticum Universum,* 5 vols. in 12, Romae, 1843-1845.

Toso, A., *Ad Codicem Iuris Canonici Commentaria Minora,* 5 vols., Romae: Marietti, 1920-1927.

Vermeersch, A.-Creusen, J., *Epitome Iuris Canonici,* 3 vols., Mechliniae-Romae: H. Dessain, Vol. I, 6 ed., 1937; Vol. II, 6 ed., 1945.

Waldron, J., *The Minister of Baptism,* The Catholic University of America Canon Law Studies, n. 170, Washington, D.C.: The Catholic University of America, 1942.

Wernz, F., *Ius Decretalium,* 6 vols., Vol. II, 3 ed., Prati, 1915.

Wernz, F.-Vidal, P., *Ius Canonicum,* 7 vols. in 8, Romae: Apud Aedes Universitatis Gregorianae, 1923-1938; Vol. II, 2 ed., 1928.

ARTICLES

Bastnagel, C., "The Parochial Vicar Substitute and the *Missa pro Populo*" —*The Jurist,* VII (1947), 64-66.

Cappello, F., "De Vicario Substituto"—*Periodica,* XIX (1930), 1*-10*.

Claeys-Boúúaert, F., "De Vicarii Substituti Constitutione ac Munere"—*Jus Pontificium,* VII (1927), 72-81.

Connell, F., "Priestly Ministry of the Essentials of Faith"—*The Ecclesiastical Review,* LXXVI (1927), 570-579.

Pointek, C., "A Gentleman's Agreement"—*The Jurist,* III (1943), 284-305.

Roelker, E. "The Vicar General and The Special Mandate"—*The Jurist,* II (1942), 346-362.

Stocchiero, J., "De Jurisdictione Vicariorum Paroecialium"—*Jus Pontificium,* XI (1931), 144-150; 221-231.

PERIODICALS

American Ecclesiastical Review, The (from Jan. 1906 to December 1943, The Ecclesiastical Review), Philadelphia, 1889-1943; Washington, D.C., 1944—.

Jus Pontificium, Romae, 1921—.

Jurist, The, Washington, D.C.: The Catholic University of America, 1941—.

Periodica de Re Canonica et Morali utili praesertim Religiosis et Missionariis, Bruges, 1905—.

ABBREVIATIONS

AAS—*Acta Apostolicae Sedis.*
AER—*The American Ecclesiastical Review.*
C.—*Codex* (Iustinianus) vel *Causa.*
c.—canon seu caput (iuris antiqui).
cc.—canones seu capita (iuris antiqui).
can.—canon (novi Codicis).
cans.—canones (novi Codicis).
Conc. Trident.— Concilium Tridentinum.
D.—*Digestum* (Iustinianum) vel *Distinctio.*
ER—*The Ecclesiastical Review.*
Fontes—*Codicis Iuris Canonici Fontes.*
Hardouin—*Conciliorum Collectio Regia Maxima.*
Mansi—*Sacrorum Conciliorum Nova et Amplissima Collectio.*
MPG—(Migne, *Patrologia Graeca*) Migne, J. P., *Patrologiae Cursus Completus, Series Graeca.*
P.C.I.—Pontificia Commissio Interpretationis.
S.C.C.—Sacra Congregatio Concilii.
S.C. de Prop. Fide—Sacra Congregatio de Propaganda Fide.
S.C. Ep. et Reg.—Sacra Congregatio Episcoporum et Regularium.
S.C.S.Off.—Sacra Congregatio Sancti Officii.
Thesaurus Resolutionum—*Thesaurus Resolutionum Sacrae Congregationis Concilii.*

BIOGRAPHICAL NOTE

Urban S. Wagner was born August 7, 1915, in Louisville, Ky. After completing his elementary education in St. Anthony's Parochial School, Louisville, Ky., he entered Mount St. Francis Pro-Seminary and College, Mount St. Francis, Indiana, in 1929. After completing the high school and two year college course, he was admitted to the Novitate of the Order of Friars Minor Conventual in 1935. He was professed in the Order September 18 of the following year, and entered Our Lady of Carey Seminary at Carey, Ohio, where he completed the course in Philosophy and Theology. He was ordained to the priesthood June 7, 1941. In September of that year he entered upon graduate studies in the School of Canon Law of the Catholic University of America, Washington, D.C. He received the Baccalaureate in Canon Law in June, 1942, and the Licentiate in Canon Law in June, 1943.

INDEX

Canon Law Studies*

1. Freriks, Rev. Celestine A., C.PP.S., J.C.D., Religious Congregations in Their External Relations, 121 pp., 1916.
2. Galliher, Rev. Daniel M., O.P., J.C.D., Canonical Elections, 117 pp., 1917.
3. Borkowski, Rev. Aurelius L., O.F.M., J.C.D., De Confraternitatibus Ecclesiasticis, 136 pp., 1918.
4. Castillo, Rev. Cayo, J.C.D., Disertacion Historico-Canonica sobre la Potestad del Cabildo en Sede Vacante o Impedida del Vicario Capitular, 99 pp., 1919 (1918).
5. Kubelbeck, Rev. William J., S.T.B., J.C.D., The Sacred Penitentiaria and Its Relation to Faculties of Ordinaries and Priests, 129 pp., 1918.
6. Petrovits, Rev. Joseph, J.C., S.T.D., J.C.D., The New Church Law on Matrimony, X-461 pp., 1919.
7. Hickey, Rev. John J., S.T.B., J.C.D., Irregularities and Simple Impediments in the New Code of Canon Law, 100 pp., 1920.
8. Klekotka, Rev. Peter J., S.T.B., J.C.D., Diocesan Consultors, 179 pp., 1920.
9. Wanenmacher, Rev. Francis, J.C.D., The Evidence in Ecclesiastical Procedure Affecting the Marriage Bond, 1920 (Printed 1935).
10. Golden, Rev. Henry Francis, J.C.D., Parochial Benefices in the New Code, IV-119 pp., 1921 (Printed 1925).
11. Koudelka, Rev. Charles J., J.C.D., Pastors, Their Rights and Duties According to the New Code of Canon Law, 211 pp., 1921.
12. Melo, Rev. Antonius, O.F.M., J.C.D., De Exemptione Regularium, X-188 pp., 1921.
13. Schaaf, Rev. Valentine Theodore, O.F.M., S.T.B., J.C.D., The Cloister, X-180 pp., 1921.
14. Burke, Rev. Thomas Joseph, S.T.D., J.C.D., Competence in Ecclesiastical Tribunals, IV-117 pp., 1922.
15. Leech, Rev. George Leo, J.C.D., A Comparative Study of the Constitution "Apostolicae Sedis" and the "Codex Juris Canonici," 179 pp., 1922.
16. Motry, Rev. Hubert Louis, S.T.D., J.C.D., Diocesan Faculties According to the Code of Canon Law, II-167 pp., 1922.
17. Murphy, Rev. George Lawrence, J.C.D., Delinquencies and Penalties in the Administration and the Reception of the Sacraments, IV-121 pp., 1923.
18. O'Reilly, Rev. John Anthony, S.T.B., J.C.D., Ecclesiastical Sepulture in the New Code of Canon Law, II-129 pp., 1923.
19. Michalicka, Rev. Wenceslas Cyrill, O.S.B., J.C.D., Judicial Procedure in Dismissal of Clerical Exempt Religious, 107 pp., 1923.
20. Dargin, Rev. Edward Vincent, S.T.B., J.C.D., Reserved Cases According to the Code of Canon Law, IV-103 pp., 1924.

* From nn. 1-100 only n. 25 is still obtainable. From n. 101 onward all numbers are available except the following: 101-114, also 116, 118, 120, 122, 123 and 162.

21. Godfrey, Rev. John A., S.T.B., J.C.D., The Right of Patronage According to the Code of Canon Law, 153 pp., 1924.
22. Hagedorn, Rev. Francis Edward, J.C.D., General Legislation on Indulgences, II-154 pp., 1924.
23. King, Rev. James Ignatius, J.C.D., The Administration of the Sacraments to Dying Non-Catholics, V-141 pp., 1924.
24. Winslow, Rev. Francis Joseph, O.F.M., J.C.D., Vicars and Prefects Apostolic, IV-149 pp., 1924.
25. Correa, Rev. Jose Servelion, S.T.L., J.C.D., La Potestad Legislativa de la Iglesia Catolica, IV-127 pp., 1925.
26. Dugan, Rev. Henry Francis, A.M., J.C.D., The Judiciary Department of the Diocesan Curia, 87 pp., 1925.
27. Keller, Rev. Charles Frederick, S.T.B., J.C.D., Mass Stipends, 167 pp., 1925.
28. Paschang, Rev. John Linus, J.C.D., The Sacramentals According to the Code of Canon Law, 129 pp., 1925.
29. Piontek, Rev. Cyrillus, O.F.M., S.T.B., J.C.D., De Inducto Exclaustrationis necnon Saecularizationis, XIII-289 pp., 1925.
30. Kearny, Rev. Richard Joseph, S.T.B., J.C.D., Sponsors at Baptism According to the Code of Canon Law, IV-127 pp., 1925.
31. Bartlett, Rev. Chester Joseph, A.M., LL.B., J.C.D., The Tenure of Parochial Property in the United States of America, V-108 pp., 1926.
32. Kilker, Rev. Adrian Jerome, J.C.D., Extreme Unction, V-425 pp., 1926.
33. McCormick, Rev. Robert Emmett, J.C.D., Confessors of Religious, VIII-266 pp., 1926.
34. Miller, Rev. Newton Thomas, J.C.D., Founded Masses According to the Code of Canon Law, VII-93 pp., 1926.
35. Roelker, Rev. Edward G., S.T.D., J.C.D., Principles of Privilege According to the Code of Canon Law, XI-166 pp., 1926.
36. Bakalarczyk, Rev. Richardus, M.I.C., J.U.D., De Novitiatu, VIII-208 pp., 1927.
37. Pizzuti, Rev. Lawrence, O.F.M., J.U.L., De Parochis Religiosis, 1927. (Not Printed.)
38. Bliley, Rev. Nicholas Martin, O.S.B., J.C.D., Altars According to the Code of Canon Law, XIX-132 pp., 1927.
39. Brown, Mr. Brendan Francis, A.B., LL.M., J.U.D., The Canonical Juristic Personality with Special Reference to its Status in the United States of America, V-212 pp., 1927.
40. Cavanaugh, Rev. William Thomas, C.P., J.U.D., The Reservation of the Blessed Sacrament, VIII-101 pp., 1927.
41. Doheny, Rev. William J., C.S.C., A.B., J.U.D., Church Property: Modes of Acquisition, X-118 pp., 1927.
42. Feldhaus, Rev. Aloysius H., C.PP.S., J.C.D., Oratories, IX-141 pp., 1927.
43. Kelly, Rev. James Patrick, A.B., J.C.D., The Jurisdiction of the Simple Confessor, X-208 pp., 1927.
44. Neuberger, Rev. Nicholas J., J.C.D., Canon 6 or the Relation of the Codex Juris Canonici to the Preceding Legislation, V-95 pp., 1927.
45. O'Keefe, Rev. Gerald Michael, J.C.D., Matrimonial Dispensations, Powers of Bishops, Priests, and Confessors, VIII-232 pp., 1927.
46. Quigley, Rev. Joseph A. M., A.B., J.C.D., Condemned Societies, 139 pp., 1927.

47. Zaplotnik, Rev. Johannes Leo, J.C.D., De Vicariis Foraneis, X-142 pp., 1927.
48. Duske, Rev. John Aloysius, A.B., J.C.D., The Canonical Status of the Orientals in the United States, VIII-196 pp., 1928.
49. Hyland, Rev. Francis Edward, J.C.D., Excommunication, Its Nature, Historical Development and Effects, VII-181 pp., 1928.
50. Reinmann, Rev. Gerald Joseph, O.M.C., J.C.D., The Third Order Secular of Saint Francis, 201 pp., 1928.
51. Schenk, Rev. Francis J., J.C.D., The Matrimonial Impediments of Mixed Religion and Disparity of Cult, XVI-318 pp., 1929.
52. Coady, Rev. John Joseph, S.T.D., J.U.D., A.M., The Appointment of Pastors, VIII-150 pp., 1929.
53. Kay, Rev. Thomas Henry, J.C.D., Competence in Matrimonial Procedure, VIII-164 pp., 1929.
54. Turner, Rev. Sidney Joseph, C.P., J.U.D., The Vow of Poverty, XLIX-217 pp., 1929.
55. Kearney, Rev. Raymond A., A.B., S.T.D., J.C.D., The Principles of Delegation, VII-149 pp., 1929.
56. Conran, Rev. Edward James, A.B., J.C.D., The Interdict, V-163 pp., 1930.
57. O'Neill, Rev. William H., J.C.D., Papal Rescripts of Favor, VII-218 pp., 1930.
58. Bastnagel, Rev. Clement Vincent, J.U.D., The Appointment of Parochial Adjutants and Assistants, XV-257 pp., 1930.
59. Ferry, Rev. William A., A.B., J.C.D., Stole Fees, V-136 pp., 1930.
60. Costello, Rev. John Michael, A.B., J.C.D., Domicile and Quasi-Domicile, VII-201 pp., 1930.
61. Kremer, Rev. Michael Nicholas, A.B., S.T.B., J.C.D., Church Support in the United States, VI-136 pp., 1930.
62. Angulo, Rev. Luis, C.M., J.C.D., Legislation de la Iglesia sobre la intencion en la application de la Santa Misa, VII-104 pp., 1931.
63. Frey, Rev. Wolfgang Norbert, O.S.B., A.B., J.C.D., The Act of Religious Profession, VIII-174 pp., 1931.
64. Roberts, Rev. James Brendan, A.B., J.C.D., The Banns of Marriage, XIV-140 pp., 1931.
66. Campagna, Rev. Angelo, Ph.D., J.U.D., Il Vicario Generale del Vescovo, VII-205 pp., 1931.
66. Campagna, Rev. Angelo, Ph.D., Il Vicario Generale del Vescovo, VII-205 pp., 1931.
67. Cox, Rev. Joseph Godfrey, A.B., J.C.D., The Administration of Seminaries, VI-124 pp., 1931.
68. Gregory, Rev. Donald J., J.U.D., The Pauline Pirivilege, XV-165 pp., 1931.
69. Donohue, Rev. John F., J.C.D., The Impediment of Crime, VII-110 pp., 1931.
70. Dooley, Rev. Eugene A., O.M.I., J.C.D., Church Law on Sacred Relics, IX-143 pp., 1931.
71. Orth, Rev. Clement Raymond, O.M.C., J.C.D., The Approbation of Religious Institutes, 171 pp., 1931.
72. Pernicone, Rev. Joseph M., A.B., J.C.D., The Ecclesiastical Prohibition of Books, XII-267 pp., 1932.
73. Clinton, Rev. Connell, A.B., J.C.D., The Paschal Precept, IX-108 pp., 1932.
74. Donnelly, Rev. Francis B., A.M., S.T.L., J.C.D., The Diocesan Synod, VIII-125 pp., 1932.

75. Torrente, Rev. Camilo, C.M.F., J.C.D., Las Procesiones Sagradas, V-145 pp., 1932.
76. Murphy, Rev. Edwin J., C.PP.S., J.C.D., Suspension Ex Informata Conscientia, XI-122 pp., 1932.
77. MacKenzie, Rev. Eric F., A.M., S.T.L., J.C.D., The Delict of Heresy in its Commission, Penalization, Absolution, VII-124 pp., 1932.
78. Lyons, Rev. Avitus E., S.T.B., J.C.D., The Collegiate Tribunal of First Instance, XI-147 pp., 1932.
79. Connolly, Rev. Thomas A., J.C.D., Appeals, XI-195 pp., 1932.
80. Sangmeister, Rev. Joseph V., A.B., J.C.D., Force and Fear as Precluding Matrimonial Consent, V-211 pp., 1932.
81. Jaeger, Rev. Leo A., A.B., J.C.D., The Administration of Vacant and Quasi-Vacant Episcopal Sees in the United States, IX-229 pp., 1932.
82. Rimlinger, Rev. Herbert T., J.C.D., Error Invalidating Matrimonial Consent, VII-79 pp., 1932.
83. Barrett, Rev. John D. M., S.S., J.C.D., A Comparative Study of the Councils of Baltimore and the Code of Canon Law, X-223 pp., 1932.
84. Carberry, Rev. John J., Ph.D., S.T.D., J.C.D., The Juridical Form of Marriage, X-177 pp., 1934.
85. Dolan, Rev. John L., A.B., J.C.D., The Defensor Vinculi, XII-157 pp., 1934.
86. Hannan, Rev. Jerome D., A.M., S.T.D., LL.B., J.C.D., The Canon Law of Wills, IX-517 pp., 1934.
87. Lemieux, Rev. Delise A., A.M., J.C.D., The Sentence in Ecclesiastical Procedure, IX-131 pp., 1934.
88. O'Rourke, Rev. James J., A.B., J.C.D., Parish Registers, VII-109 pp., 1934.
89. Timlin, Rev. Bartholomew, O.F.M., A.M., J.C.D., Conditional Matrimonial Consent, X-381 pp., 1934.
90. Wahl, Rev. Francis X., A.B., J.C.D., The Matrimonial Impediments of Consanguinity and Affinity, VI-125 pp., 1934.
91. White, Rev. Robert J., A.B., LL.B., S.T.B., J.C.D., Canonical Ante-Nuptial Promises and the Civil Law, VI-152 pp., 1934.
92. Herrera, Rev. Antonio Parra, O.C.D., J.C.D., Legislacion Ecclesiastica sobra el Ayuno y la Abstinencia, XI-191 pp., 1935.
93. Kennedy, Rev. Edwin J., J.C.D., The Special Matrimonial Process in Cases of Evident Nullity, X-165 pp., 1935.
94. Manning, Rev. John J., A.B., J.C.D., Presumption of Law in Matrimonial Procedure, XI-111 pp., 1935.
95. Moeder, Rev. John M., J.C.D., The Proper Bishop for Ordination and Dimissorial Letters, VII-135 pp., 1935.
96. O'Mara, Rev. William A., A.B., J.C.D., Canonical Causes for Matrimonial Dispensations, IX-155 pp., 1935.
97. Reilly, Rev. Peter, J.C.D., Residence of Pastors, IX-81 pp., 1935.
98. Smith, Rev. Mariner T., O.P., S.T.Lr., J.C.D., The Penal Law for Religious, VIII-169 pp., 1935.
99. Whalen, Rev. Donald W., A.M., J.C.D., The Value of Testimonial Evidence in Matrimonial Procedure, XIII-297 pp., 1935.
100. Cleary, Rev. Joseph F., J.C.D., Canonical Limitations on the Alienation of Church Property, VIII-141 pp., 1936.
101. Glynn, Rev. John C., J.C.D., The Promoter of Justice, XX-337 pp., 1936.
102. Brennan, Rev. James H., S.S., M.A., S.T.B., J.C.D., The Simple Convalidation of Marriage, VI-135 pp., 1937.

103. Brunini, Rev. Joseph Bernard, J.C.D., The Clerical Obligations of Canons 139 and 142, X-121 pp., 1937.
104. Connor, Rev. Maurice, A.B., J.C.D., The Administrative Removal of Pastors, VIII-159 pp., 1937.
105. Guilfoyle, Rev. Merlin Joseph, J.C.D., Custom, XI-144 pp., 1937.
106. Hughes, Rev. James Austin, A.B., A.M., J.C.D., Witnesses in Criminal Trials of Clerics, IX-140 pp., 1937.
107. Janson, Rev. Raymond J., A.B., S.T.L., J.C.D., Canonical Provisions for Catechetical Instruction, VII-153 pp., 1937.
108. Kealy, Rev. John James, A.B., J.C.D., The Introductory Libellus in Church Court Procedure, XI-121 pp., 1937.
109. McManus, Rev. James Edward, C.SS.R., J.C.D., The Administration of Temporal Goods in Religious Institutes, XVI-196 pp., 1937.
110. Moriarity, Rev. Eugene James, J.C.D., Oaths in Ecclesiastical Courts, X-115 pp., 1937.
111. Rainer, Rev. Eligius George, C.SS.R., J.C.D., Suspension of Clerics, XVII-249 pp., 1937.
112. Reilly, Rev. Thomas F., C.SS.R., J.C.D., Visitation of Religious, VI-195 pp., 1938.
113. Moriarity, Rev. Francis E., C.SS.R., J.C.D., The Extraordinary Absolution from Censures, XV-334 pp., 1938.
114. Connolly, Rev. Nicholas P., J.C.D., The Canonical Erection of Parishes, X-132 pp., 1938.
115. Donovan, Rev. James Joseph, J.C.D., The Pastor's Obligation in Prenuptial Investigation, XII-322 pp., 1938.
116. Harrigan, Rev. Robert J., M.A., S.T.B., J.C.D., The Radical Sanation of Invalid Marriages, VIII-208 pp., 1938.
117. Boffa, Rev. Conrad Humbert, J.C.D., Canonical Provisions for Catholic Schools, VII-211 pp., 1939.
118. Parsons, Rev. Anscar John, O.M.Cap., J.C.D., Canonical Elections, XII-236 pp., 1939.
119. Reilly, Rev. Edward Michael, A.B., J.C.D., The General Norms of Dispensation, XII-156 pp., 1939.
120. Ryan, Rev. Gerald Aloysius, A.B., J.C.D., Principles of Episcopal Jurisdiction, XII-172 pp., 1939.
121. Burton, Rev. Francis James, C.S.C., A.B., J.C.D., A Commentary on Canon 1125, X-222 pp., 1940.
122. Miaskiewicz, Rev. Francis Sigismund, J.C.D., Supplied Jurisdiction According to Canon 209, XII-340 pp., 1940.
123. Rice, Rev. Patrick William, A.B., J.C.D., Proof of Death in Prenuptial Investigation, VIII-156 pp., 1940.
124. Anglin, Rev., Thomas Francis, M.S., J.C.D., The Eucharistic Fast, VIII-183 pp., 1941.
125. Coleman, Rev. John Jerome, J.C.D., The Minister of Confirmation, VI-153 pp., 1941.
126. Downs, Rev. John Emmanuel, A.B., J.C.D., The Concept of Clerical Immunity, XI-163 pp., 1941.
127. Esswein, Rev. Anthony Albert, J.C.D., Extrajudicial Penal Powers of Ecclesiastical Superiors, X-144 pp., 1941.
128. Farrell, Rev. Benjamin Francis, M.A., S.T.L., J.C.D., The Rights and Duties of the Local Ordinary Regarding Congregations of Women Religious of Pontifical Approval, V-195 pp., 1941.
129. Feeney, Rev. Thomas John, A.B., S.T.L., J.C.D., Restitutio in Integrum, VI-169 pp., 1941.

130. Findlay, Rev. Stephen William, O.S.B., A.B., J.C.D., Canonical Norms Governing the Deposition and Degradation of Clerics, XVII-279 pp., 1941.
131. Goodwine, Rev. John, A.B., S.T.L., J.C.D., The Right of the Church to Acquire Property, VIII-119 pp., 1941.
132. Heston, Rev. Edward Louis, C.S.C., Ph.D., S.T.D., J.C.D., The Alienation of Church Property in the United States, XII-222 pp., 1941.
133. Hogan, Rev. James John, A.B., S.T.L., J.C.D., Judicial Advocates and Procurators, XIII-200 pp., 1941.
134. Kealy, Rev. Thomas M., A.B., Litt.B., J.C.D., Dowry of Women Religious, IX-152 pp., 1941.
135. Keene, Rev. Michael James, O.S.B., J.C.D., Religious Ordinaries and Canon 198, V-164 pp., 1942.
136. Kerin, Rev. Charles A., S.S., M.A., S.T.B., J.C.D., The Privation of Christian Burial, XVI-279 pp., 1941.
137. Louis, Rev. William Francis, M.A., J.C.D., Diocesan Archives, X-101 pp., 1941.
138. McDevitt, Rev. Gilbert Joseph, A.B., J.C.D., Legitimacy and Legitimation, X-247 pp., 1941.
139. McDonough, Rev. Thomas Joseph, A.B., J.C.D., Apostolic Administrators, X-217 pp., 1941.
140. Meier, Rev. Carl Anthony, A.B., J.C.D., Penal Administrative Procedure Against Negligent Pastors, XI-240 pp., 1941.
141. Schmidt, Rev. John Rogg, A.B., J.C.D., The Principles of Authentic Interpretation in Canon 17 of the Code of Canon Law, XII-331 pp., 1941.
142. Slafkosky, Rev. Andrew Leonard, A.B., J.C.D., The Canonical Episcopal Visitations of the Diocese, X-197 pp., 1941.
143. Swoboda, Rev. Innocent Robert, O.F.M., J.C.D., Ignorance in Relation to the Imputability of Delicts, IX-271 pp., 1941.
144. Dubé, Rev. Arthur Joseph, A.B., J.C.D., The General Principles for the Reckoning of Time in Canon Law, VIII-299 pp., 1941.
145. McBride, Rev. James T., A.B., J.C.D., Incardination and Excardination of Seculars, XX-585 pp., 1941.
146. Król, Rev. John T., J.C.D., The Defendant in Ecclesiastical Trials, XII-207 pp., 1942.
147. Comyns, Rev. Joseph J., C.SS.R., A.B., J.C.D., Papal and Episcopal Administration of Church Property, XIV-155 pp., 1942.
148. Barry, Rev. Garrett Francis, O.M.I., J.C.D., Violation of the Cloister, XII-260 pp., 1942.
149. Bolduc, Rev. Gatien, C.S.V., A.B., S.T.L., J.C.D., Les Études dans les Religions Cléricales, VIII-155 pp., 1942.
150. Boyle, Rev. David John, M.A., J.C.D., The Juridic Effects of Moral Certitude on Pre-Nuptial Guarantees, XII-188 pp., 1942.
151. Canavan, Rev. Walter Joseph, M.A., Litt.D., J.C.D., The Profession of Faith, XII-143 pp., 1942.
152. Desrochers, Rev. Bruno, A.B., Ph.L., S.T.B., J.C.D., Le Premier Concile Plénier de Québec et le Code de Droit Canonique, XIV-186 pp., 1942.
153. Dillon, Rev. Robert Edward, A.B., J.C.D., Common Law Marriage, X-148 pp., 1942.
154. Dodwell, Rev. Edward John, Ph.D., S. T. B., J.C.D., The Time and Place for the Celebration of Marriage, X-156 pp., 1942.

155. Donnellan, Rev. Thomas Andrew, A.B., J.C.D., The Obligation of the Missa pro Populo, VII-131 pp., 1942.
156. Eltz, Rev. Louis Anthony, A.B., J.C.D., Cooperation in Crime, XII-208 pp., 1942.
157. Gass, Rev. Sylvester Francis, M.A., J.C.D., Ecclesiastical Pensions, XI-206 pp., 1942.
158. Guiniven, Rev. John Joseph, C.SS.R., J.C.D., The Precept of Hearing Mass, XIV-188 pp., 1942.
159. Gulcynski, Rev. John Theophilus, J.C.D., The Desecration and Violation of Churches, X-126 pp., 1942.
160. Hammill, Rev. John Leo, M.A., J.C.D., The Obligations of the Traveler According to Canon 14, VIII-204 pp., 1942.
161. Haydt, Rev. John Joseph, A.B., J.C.D., Reserved Benefices, XI-148 pp., 1942.
162. Huser, Rev. Roger John, O.F.M., A.B., J.C.D., The Crime of Abortion in Canon Law, XII-187 pp., 1942.
163. Kearney, Rev. Francis Patrick, A.B., S.T.L., J.C.D., The Principles of Canon 1127, X-162 pp., 1942.
164. Linahen, Rev. Leo James, S.T.L., J.C.D., De Absolutione Complicis In Peccato Turpi, 114., 1942.
165. McCloskey, Rev. Joseph Aloysius, A.B., J.C.D., The Subject of Ecclesiastical Law According to Canon 12, XVII-246 pp., 1942.
166. O'Neill, Rev. Francis Joseph, C.SS.R., J.C.D., The Dismissal of Religious in Temporary Vows, XIII-220 pp., 1942.
167. Prince, Rev. John Edward, A.B., S.T.B., J.C.D., The Diocesan Chancellor, X-136 pp., 1942.
168. Riesner, Rev. Albert Joseph, C.SS.R., J.C.D., Apostates and Fugitives from Religious Institutes, IX-168 pp., 1942.
169. Stenger, Rev. Joseph Bernard, J.C.D., The Mortgaging of Church Property, 186 pp., 1942.
170. Waldron, Rev. Joseph Francis, A.B., J.C.D., The Minister of Baptism, XII-197 pp., 1942.
171. Willett, Rev. Robert Albert, J.C.D., The Probative Value of Documents in Ecclesiastical Trials. X-124 pp., 1942.
172. Woeber, Rev. Edward Martin, M.A., J.C.D., The Interpellations, XII-161 pp., 1942.
173. Benko, Rev. Matthew Aloysius, O.S.B., M.A., J.C.D., The Abbot *Nullius*, XVI-148 pp., 1943.
174. Christ, Rev. Joseph James, M.A., S.T.L., J.C.D., Dispensation from Vindicative Penalties, XIII-285 pp., 1943.
175. Clancy, Rev. Patrick M. J., O.P., A.B., S.T. Lr., J.C.D., The Local Religious Superior, X-229 pp., 1943.
176. Clarke, Rev. Thomas James, J.C.D., Parish Societies, XII-147 pp., 1943.
177. Connolly, Rev. John Patrick, S.T.L., J.C.D., Synodal Examiners, and Parish Priest Consultors, X-223 pp., 1943.
178. Drumm, Rev. William Martin, A.B., J.C.D., Hospital Chaplains, XII-175 pp., 1943.
179. Flanagan, Rev. Bernard Joseph, A.B., S.T.L., J.C.D., The Canonical Erection of Religious Houses. X-147 pp., 1943.
180. Kelleher, Rev. Stephen Joseph, A.B., S.T.B., J.C.D., Discussions with Non-Catholics: Canonical Legislation, X-93 pp., 1943.
181. Lewis, Rev. Gordian, C.P., J.C.D., Chapters in Religious Institutes, XII-169 pp., 1943.

182. MARX, REV. ADOLPH, J.C.D., The Declaration of Nullity of Marriages Contracted Outside the Church, X-151 pp., 1943.
183. MATULENAS, REV. RAYMOND ANTHONY, O.S.B., A.B., J.C.D., Communication, a Source of Privileges, XII-225 pp., 1943.
184. O'LEARY, REV. CHARLES GERARD, C.SS.R., J.C.D., Religious Dismissed After Perpetual Profession, X-213 pp., 1943.
185. POWER, REV. CORNELIUS MICHAEL, J.C.D., The Blessing of Cemeteries, XII-231 pp., 1943.
186. SHUHLER, REV. RALPH VINCENT, O.S.A., J.C.D., Privileges of Religious to Absolve and Dispense, XII-195 pp., 1943.
187. ZIOLKOWSKI, REV. THADDEUS STANISLAUS, A.B., J.C.D., The Consecration and Blessing of Churches, XII-151 pp., 1943.
188. HENEGHAN, REV. JOHN JOSEPH, S.T.D., J.C.D., The Marriages of Unworthy Catholics: Canons 1065 and 1066, XVI-213 pp., 1944.
189. CARROLL, REV. COLEMAN FRANCIS, M.A., S.T.L., J.C.L., Charitable Institutions.
190. CIESLUK, REV. JOSEPH EDWARD, PH.B., S.T.L., J.C.L., National Parishes in the United States.
191. COBURN, REV. VINCENT PAUL, A.B., J.C.D., Marriages of Conscience, XII-172 pp., 1944.
192. CONNORS, REV. CHARLES PAUL, C.S.SP., A.B., J.C.D., Extra-Juridical Procurators in the Code of Canon Law, X-94 pp., 1944.
193. COYLE, REV. PAUL RAYMOND, A.B., J.C.D., Judicial Exceptions, IX-142 pp., 1944.
194. FAIR, REV. BARTHOLOMEW FRANCIS, A.B., S.T.L., J.C.D., The Impediment of Abduction, XII-122 pp., 1944.
195. GALLAGHER, REV. THOMAS RAPHAEL, O.P., A.B., S.T.LR., J.C.D., The Examination of the Qualities of the Ordinand, X-166 pp., 1944.
196. GANNON, REV. JOHN MARK, S.T.L., J.C.D., The Interstices Required for the Promotion to Orders, VII-100 pp., 1944.
197. GOLDSMITH, REV. J. WILLIAM, B.C.S., S.T.L., J.C.D., The Competence of Church and State Over Marriage—Disputed Points, X-128 pp., 1944.
198. GOODWINE, REV. JOSEPH GERARD, A.B., S.T.B., J.C.D., The Reception of Converts, XIV-326 pp., 1944.
199. KOWALSKI, REV. ROMUALD EUGENE, O.F.M., A.B., J.C.D., Sustenance of Religious Houses of Regulars, X-174 pp., 1944.
200. MCCOY, REV. ALAN EDWARD, O.F.M., J.C.D., Force and Fear in Relation to Delictual Imputability and Penal Responsibility, XII-160 pp., 1944.
201. MCDEVITT, REV. VINCENT JOHN, PH.B., S.T.L., J.C.L., Perjury.
202. MARTIN, REV. THOMAS OWEN, PH.D., S.T.D., J.C.D., Adverse Possession, Prescription and Limitation of Actions: The Canonical "Praescriptio," XX-208 pp., 1944.
203. MIKLOSOVIC, REV. PAUL JOHN, A.B., J.C.L., Attempted Marriages and Their Consequent Juridic Effects.
204. MUNDY, REV. THOMAS MAURICE, A.B., S.T.L., J.C.D., The Union of Parishes, X-164 pp., 1944.
205. O'DEA, REV. JOHN COYLE, A.B., J.C.D., The Matrimonial Impediment of Nonage, VIII-126 pp., 1944.
206. OLALIA, REV. ALEXANDER AYSON, S.T.L., J.C.D., A Comparative Study of the Christian Constitution of States and the Constitution of the Philippine Commonwealth, XII-136 pp., 1944.
207. POISSON, REV. PIERRE-MARIE, C.S.C., A.B., PH.L., TH.L., J.C.L., Droits Patrimoniaux des Maisons et des Eglises Religieuses.

208. Stadalnikas, Rev. Casimir Joseph, M.I.C., J.C.D., Reservation of Censures, X-141 pp., 1944.
209. Sullivan, Rev. Eugene Henry, S.T.L., J.C.D., Proof of the Reception of the Sacraments, X-165 pp., 1944.
210. Vaughan, Rev. William Edward, J.C.D., Constitutions for Diocesan Courts, X-210 pp., 1944.
211. Paro, Rev. Gino, S.T.D., J.C.L., The Right of Apostolic Delegation.
212. Balzer, Rev. Ralph Francis, C.P., J.C.D., The Computation of Time in a Canonical Novitiate, X-227 pp., 1945.
213. Dougherty, Rev. John Whelan, A.B., S.T.L., J.C.D., De Inquisitione Speciali, XII-195 pp., 1945.
214. Dziob, Rev. Michael Walter, J.C.D., The Sacred Congregation for the Oriental Church, XII-181 pp., 1945.
215. Eidenschink, Rev. John Albert, O.S.B., B.A., J.C.D., The Election of Bishops in the Letters of Pope Gregory the Great, VII-200 pp., 1945.
216. Gill, Rev. Nicholas, C.P., J.C.D., The Spiritual Prefect in Clerical Religious Houses of Study, X-140 pp., 1945.
217. Hynes, Rev. Harry Gerard, S.T.L., J.C.D., The Privileges of Cardinals, XII-183 pp., 1945.
218. McDevitt, Rev. Gerald Vincent, S.T.L., J.C.D., The Renunciation of an Ecclesiastical Office, XIV-179 pp., 1945.
219. Manning, Rev. Joseph Leroy, J.C.D., The Free Conferral of Offices, VIII-116 pp., 1945.
220. Meyer, Rev. Louis G., O.S.B., A.B., S.T.B., J.C.D., Alms-gathering by Religious, XII-163 pp., 1945.
221. O'Donnell, Rev. Cletus Francis, M.A., J.C.D., The Marriage of Minors, XII-268 pp., 1945.
222. Prunskis, Rev. Joseph, J.C.D., Comparative Law, Ecclesiastical and Civil, in Lithuanian Concordat, X-161 pp., 1945.
223. Sweeney, Rev. Francis Patrick, C.SS.R., J.C.D., The Reduction of Clerics to the Lay State, X-199 pp., 1945.
224. Vogelpohl, Rev. Henry John, J.C.D., The Simple Impediments to Holy Orders, XVI-190 pp., 1945.
225. Brockhaus, Rev. Thomas Aquinas, O.S.B., J.C.D., Religious who are known as *Conversi*, X-127 pp., 1945.
226. Griese, Rev. N. Orville, S.T.D., J.C.D., The Marriage Contract and the Procreation of Offspring, XVI-224 pp., 1946.
227. Boudreaux, Rev. Warren Louis, J.C.L., The *"ab acatholicis nati" of* Canon 1099, § 2.
228. Bowe, Rev. Thomas Joseph, A.B., J.C.L., Religious Superioresses.
229. Diederichs, Rev. Michael Ferdinand, S.C.J., J.C.D., The Jurisdiction of the Latin Ordinaries over their Oriental Subjects, XIV-153 pp., 1946.
230. Dingman, Rev. Maurice John, A.B., S.T.L., J.C.L., The Plaintiff in Contentious Trials.
231. Frison, Rev. Basil, C.M.F., M.Mus., J.C.D., The Retroactivity of Law, X-221 pp., 1946.
232. Galvin, Rev. William Anthony, M.A., J.C.D., The Administrative Transfer of Pastors, XII-288 pp., 1946.
233. Goracy, Rev. Joseph C., J.C.D., The Diriment Matrimonial Impediment of Major Orders.
234. Hale, Rev. Joseph Francis, M.A., S.T.L., J.C.D., The Pastor of Burial.
235. Henry, Rev. Joseph Arthur, A.B., J.C.D., The Mass and Holy Communion: Inter-Ritual Law, XII-138 pp., 1946.

236. Lindenberger, Rev. Herbert, C.PP.S., J.C.D., The False Denunciation of an Innocent Confessor.
237. Lowry, Rev. James Martin, A.B., J.C.D., Dispensation from Private Vows, XII-216 pp., 1946.
238. Lynch, Rev. George Edward, A.B., S.T.L., J.C.D., Coadjutors and Auxiliaries of Bishops, X-107 pp., 1947.
239. Lynch, Rev. Timothy, M.S.SS.T., J.C.D., Contracts between Bishops and Religious Congregations, XIV-232 pp., 1946.
240. McClunn, Rev. Justin David, A.B., S.T.L., J.C.D., Administrative Recourse, VII-142 pp., 1946.
241. Lohmuller, Rev. Martin Nicholas, A.B., J.C.D., The Promulgation of Law, XII-140 pp., 1947.
242. McGrath, Rev. James, A.B., J.C.D., The Privilege of the Canon, XII-156 pp., 1946.
243. Marbach, Rev. Joseph Francis, A.B., J.C.D., Marriage Legislation for the Catholics of the Oriental Rites in the United States and Canada, XIV-314 pp., 1946.
244. Shimkus, Rev. Bernard Aloysius, A.B., J.C.L., The Determination and Transfer of Rite.
245. Smith, Rev. Vincent Michael, A.B., S.T.L., J.C.L., Ignorance Affecting Matrimonial Consent.
246. Wachtrle, Rev. Paul Anthony, A.B., J.C.L., The Baptism of the Children of Non-Catholics.
247. Crotty, Rev. Matthew M., J.C.L., The Recipient of First Holy Communion.
248. Eagleton, Rev. George, J.C.L., The Quinquennial Faculties, Formula IV.
249. Gibbons, Rev. Marion L., C.M., J.C.L., Domicile of the Wife Unlawfully Separated from Her Husband.
250. Kelley, Rev. Bernard M., J.C.L., The Functions Reserved to Pastors.
251. Kilcullen, Rev. Thomas J., J.C.L., The Collegiate Moral Person as Party Litigant.
252. Lafontaine, Rev. Germain, W. F., J.C.L., Relations Canoniques entre le Missionaire et Ses Superieurs.
253. Lane, Rev. Loras T., J.C.L., Matrimonial Procedure in Ordinary Court of Second Instance.
254. Lover, Rev. James F., C.Ss.R., J.C.L., The Master of Novices.
255. McNicholas, Rev. Timothy J., J.C.L., The *Septimae Manus* Witness.
256. Marositz, Rev. Joseph J., M.S.C., J.C.L., Obligations and Privileges of Religious Promoted to the Episcopal or Cardinalitial Dignities.
257. Murphy, Rev. Francis J., J.C.L., Legislative Powers of the Provincial Council.
258. O'Brien, Rev. Romaeus W., O.Carm., J.C.L., The Provincial Superior in Religious Orders of Men.
259. Pfaller, Rev. Benedict A., O.S.B., J.C.L., The *ipso facto* Effected Dismissal of Religious.
260. Popek, Rev. Alphonse S., J.C.L., The Rights and Obligations of Metropolitans.
261. Ristuccia, Rev. Bernard J., C.M., J.C.L., Quasi-Religious.
262. Sonntag, Rev. Nathaniel L., O.F.M.,Cap., J.C.L., Consorship of Special Classes of Books.
263. Stadler, Rev. Joseph N., J.C.L., Frequent Holy Communion.
264. Szal, Rev. Ignatius J., J.C.L., The Communication of Catholics with Schismatics.
265. Wagner, Rev. Urban S., O.F.M.,Conv., J.C.L., Parochial Substitute Vicars and Supplying Priests.

www.ingramcontent.com/pod-product-compliance
Lightning Source LLC
LaVergne TN
LVHW050207080826
844660LV00012B/374

* 9 7 8 0 8 1 3 2 2 4 4 3 5 *